A Journey of Troubles

By
Thomas McNamee

MAPLE
PUBLISHERS

A Journey of Troubles

Author: Thomas McNamee

Copyright © 2026 Thomas McNamee

The right of Thomas McNamee to be identified as author of this work has been asserted by the author in accordance with section 77 and 78 of the Copyright, Designs and Patents Act 1988.

First Published in 2026

ISBN 978-1-83538-909-6 (Paperback)
　　 978-1-83538-910-2 (E-Book)

Book cover design and Book layout by:
　　White Magic Studios
　　www.whitemagicstudios.co.uk

Published by:
　　Maple Publishers
　　Fairbourne Drive, Atterbury,
　　Milton Keynes,
　　MK10 9RG, UK
　　www.maplepublishers.com

A CIP catalogue record for this title is available from the British Library.

All rights reserved. No part of this book may be reproduced or translated in any form or by any means, electronic or mechanical, including photocopying, recording or by any information storage and retrieval system without written permission from the author.

This book is a memoir. It reflects the author's recollections of experiences over time. Some names and characteristics have been changed, some events have been compressed, and some dialogues have been recreated, and the Publisher hereby disclaims any responsibility for them.

CONTENTS

A Journey of Troubles 5

Chapter 1 – Growing up in sweet Strabane 6

Chapter 2 – The cup final 9

Chapter 3 – King of the Gypsies 12

Chapter 4 – The uncles from hell 15

Chapter 5 – Showdown at the school 18

Chapter 6 – A working man 22

Chapter 7 – The 20 Pence Park Scandal 25

Chapter 8 – Birth of the Siontists 29

Chapter 9 – Ways of the guitar 33

Chapter 10 – In defence of a friend 38

Chapter 11 – The big contest and Ben's distraction 43

Chapter 12 – Sayonara to the Siontists 48

Chapter 13 – Discovered by the Playboys 52

Chapter 14 – The Irish fighter pilot and Gaeltacht gibberish 56

Chapter 15 – Save Stinker 62

Chapter 16 – Stinker in London 66

Chapter 17 – God Save the Queen 71

Chapter 18 – Another Boomin' Christmas 74

Chapter 19 – The shoe-shit incident 79

Chapter 20 – The 'panting dogs' and the dead dog 84

Chapter 21 – Physical Love 91

Chapter 22 – Battered by the barracks 95
Chapter 23 – Meeting Mum 101
Chapter 24 – A Glass Shave 106
Chapter 25 – Just a Blow-in 110
Chapter 26 – My Childhood 115
Chapter 27 – Dunloy on the 12th 119
Chapter 28 – It's a Beautiful Day? 123
Chapter 29 – The trip to Pissnaskea 129
Chapter 30 – Losing Uncle Bernard 133
Chapter 31 – Along came Carly 137
Chapter 32 – The worst chapter of our lives 140
Chapter 33 – Goodbye to Mum 144
Chapter 34 – The Pompous Priest 148
Chapter 35 – The Gutter Cowboys 152
Chapter 36 – Somehow still standing 156
Chapter 37 – Dad's Final Chapter 161

A Journey of Troubles

This work is dedicated to a man who during his lifetime faced waves of adversity and life challenges that would vanquish the most steadfast of men. What these challenges were exactly I will divulge as we progress further through this narrative. He was a son, husband, father and perhaps most memorably; a musician. He and his trusted abilities with the guitar took him on a journey from the most southern parts of Ireland to the highlands of Scotland where he and his fellow Playboys (name of the band) cemented a name for themselves. All of this took place against the overbearing darkness of the Troubles and the heavy presence of sectarianism that so engulfed the communities of Northern Ireland. One could arguably say that it warped the mindsets of the region's inhabitants as politicians and campaigners spat their verbal poison that embedded itself into the attitudes of the people of Northern Ireland and would continue to rear its ugly head throughout my dad's life as well as to some degree my own. I can only hope that through this work that I can do justice to my dad's life story, and that the fragmented recollections he told me about in his later years can be pieced together to form a competent retelling of his journey through life that will tap into your emotions and leave you; the reader, experiencing feelings of happiness and humour but also sympathy and sadness as we embark on the fascinating adventure that was my dad's turbulent and intriguing life.

Chapter 1

Growing up in sweet Strabane

My father was born in the year 1950. He was the oldest of three siblings. He little sister was called Mary and his brother was called Gerry. They lived on the family farm with their parents Susan and Thomas, whom I am named after. His father was an electrician. They lived in a small cottage that had shoots of green foliage intertwined with the brickwork of the house. Just outside the front door was small circular garden that had lilies, daffodils and pink roses which were tended to lovingly by his mother whenever the sun shone. Around the back was a small greenhouse where tomatoes and strawberries were grown and it was his father's job to oversee their progress. Their garden really stood out under the splendour of the summer and had an almost Eden-like quality as the greenery shimmered in the sun's basking glow. The serenity was added to by the sweet tweeting of nearby birds who flocked to feast on the seeds left out for them.

Directly to the left of the house and over the short, trimmed hedges was a large, open field, which during dad's childhood years was occupied by members of the travelling community. Often as a boy dad would cut through this field on his way to school and developed a reasonably amicable relationship with the gypsies that lived there. He told me that they could be a bit wary of outsiders or 'gorgas' as they were known to be called, but accepted my dad into their fold as he would bring them leftover butter, bread, jam and milk whenever there was any going spare. One of the gypsies he was particularly friendly with was a young boy called Sean. Sean was what you would describe as a very rough and ready character. He wore a thin white shirt that had two green stripes which was always covered in dirt.

He also never seemed to have any shoes on, and his feet were always a dark brown colour as they were caked in dirt when he waded through the mucky fields when playing with my dad as they merrily pretended to be Cowboys and Indians.

To get into the town square, where my dad was often sent to pick up groceries was a five-minute bike ride. Usually, he would stop into McIlveney's butchers to pick up a slab of meat or some sausages. Ainsley McIlveney was the owner. He was a portly fellow with bright red cheeks and very hairy arms that could be seen protruding from his rolled-up sleeves. You could describe him as a gentle giant that always had a smile on his face as he greeted my dad. "How's the clan keeping?" he would ask as he turned his back to noisily chop up some meat. "Yeah, good thank" my dad would reply, "sister's doing well in school and mum and dad are managing alright." "Good, good" he would boom out from within that big belly of his, "tell them I was asking for them." When you continued for about 2 miles down the beaten town path there was a small collection of shrubbery that when passed through led out towards a beautiful lake that sparkled and glistened during those happy summer days. Now, my dad was not much of a swimmer, but he and his friends often came here to skip rocks and relax in the stifling heat.

Charlie attended school with his 4 close friends, Ted, Peter, Stephen and Liam. Stephen was a skinny lad with a freckly face. His school blazer hung about him like a cloak and always walked with his hands in his pockets with a confident stride. Peter was the tallest of the group. He had straight blonde hair and a fringe that was a bit too long and kept dangling over his eyes and that he was forever blowing out of his eyeline. Ted had a skin-tight trim and hairy eyebrows. He was nicknamed the 'caveman' by those at school, not only because of his neanderthal like appearance but also because of the way he slouched when he walked. Finally, there was Liam 'Stinker' McAuley. The nickname is pretty self-explanatory.

Stinker was a large heavy set fellow with glasses but had an uncanny ability to stand up acrobatically on his hands with his feet pointed in the hair, a trick that would win him many a bar bet in the coming years. Together the five of them enjoyed the simple pleasures of a childhood spent mostly outdoors, of course these years being decades before satellite TVs or Xboxes and Playstations became a part of mainstream society. One of their favourite past times was playing 'conkers'. They would each explore the fertile forest and nearby fields, looking for the right conker that would see them hailed as the conkers champion.

Once they had found their chosen weapon, they would each get a piece of string and tie a knot that allowed the conker to dangle on the end of the string. They would then each take turns to thrust their conker to collide with their opponent's. The winner was whoever's conquer managed to shatter their challenger's. They also didn't let any spare scraps they came across go to waste. One day as they were walking by the old dumping grounds, they came across a large set of cardboard boxes and hopping of the wired fence, took them for themselves and built a small fort that they spent many a day hanging out within.

Charlie wasn't necessarily the most academic of figures, but he excelled at sports and was a key member of the school basketball team and competed in soccer teams both inside and outside of school and the high jump. In fact, he was selected to represent his school in the high jump championships in England, but his uncles who he lived with at the time and who were utterly horrible men that I will come to later, refused to give him permission. Charlie, as you probably have realised by now, was a very active child and was forever rushing through life, taking on all opportunities to prove himself physically and showcase his talents in athleticism. His first opportunity for sporting glory came with his local soccer team: Strabane Juniors FC, as they reached the regional cup final and with Charlie's lightning pace they felt they had a great chance of achieving glory and cementing themselves as triumphant local heroes within their community.

Chapter 2

The cup final

Charlie sat in the worn-out changing room, hands clasped and knees jangling. This was the biggest moment of his fledgling sports career, the regional cup final. Charlie played on the left wing and was doing his level best to stay focused as coach McCullagh, a tall man wearing a blue cap and tracksuit with a stern face and lowered brow gave out his final instructions to the lads. "Right boys", he announced "you are going up against a side that are taller and possibly stronger than you. So keep the ball on the ground and don't get lured into a physical match up with these chaps. Attack their full backs and exploit their lack of pace out wide. Now let's go!" And so the young bucks marched out onto the hallow turf against the Millside boys. Coach McCullagh was not exaggerating when he said they were a taller and stronger side. "They looked about 18" Charlie told me, "And some of them already had moustaches!".

Thus, the whistle blew, and they were off, Charlie stayed out wide as instructed and attacked the Millside right back by utilising his speed to leave him in knots. However, the opposition soon got wise to my dad's efforts and gave him some 'special' attention that came in the form of some hard-hitting tackles which the ref was more than happy to allow slide without interference. "Fuck sake, ref" coach McCullagh barked "they've been hacking at him all game!" Despite the extra focus that Millside were paying Charlie, he still managed to allude the defenders on more than one occasion and crossed a number of neat balls into the box but to no avail as the centre forward Marty couldn't quite get on the end of one. It was 0-0 at half time and coach McCullagh was pleased with his side's showing. "Right lads, the game is ours to seize here in the second half, keep your focus and continue the sharp triangles of passing we've been working on in training, that way we'll wear them down as the game progresses." All seemed to be falling into place in the second half as the Strabane men attacked their beleaguered opponents and came close as a strike from midfield shaved the Millside crossbar.

Their hard work and persistence would pay dividends as Oscar Simmons, a short maverick midfielder lashed one in from just outside the box. The roars went up from the Strabane end and coach McCullagh slid on his knees, knocking over a crate of water bottles. "Get in there!" he cheered as he punched the air in delight. Unfortunately, though, that is as close as they would come as the game would swing in a moment of madness. One of Strabane's central midfielders was a real hot head, Derek the Destroyer he was known as who had already been sent off 4 times this season was on a yellow card when he lunged in, studs showing and cleaned out the Millside forward. The ref had no choice. He brandished the red, "On your bike, Derek" he bellowed. "No, on YOUR bike ref!" Derek exclaimed in return and planted a Zidane-esque headbutt into the ref's mid-drift. He would subsequently be banned from playing footy for a year and Strabane would go on to lose the final 1-2. Charlie was a mixture of disappointed and angry.

How stupid could Derek be? Coach McCullagh was equally as seething as he burst into the changing room, "I know I shouldn't have started that hothead!" he panted as he strode up and down the changing room in an inconsolable rage. "Where is that useless fucker?" he shrieked "All that work, all that effort and he goes and clocks the ref!" The rest of the lads sat in abject silence. "Think he's set off home, coach" one of the boys whimpered, they were all left feeling numb from the pain of the cup final defeat. Outside the changing room one could hear the cheers of "Champeones! Champeones! Oh, le, Oh, le, Oh, le!" from the Millside contingent. Charlie trudged home in despair, some of the supporters who were walking home offered a consoling pat on the back. "Cheer up, laddie "Mr Scott, the local postie uttered. "I thought you played a bloody good game". A well known elder of the town called Harold came by slowly with his walking cane sinking into the greenery beneath his feet. "That ref was a complete joke" he said, shaking his cane angrily "though that young Derek was a flaming idiot for getting himself sent off like that!" Charlie quietly thanked the two men and meandered his way back to the homestead. Little did he know that this disappointment was to be a minor setback compared to the obstacles that life strewn in his path in the coming years.

Chapter 3

King of the Gypsies

One day, Charlie and Sean were outside painting a makeshift shed that Sean's father Michael had set up. Michael O'Reilly was arguably the most respected man amongst the local gypsy community. At the risk of sounding like I'm stereotyping, Michael; like nearly all gypsy men, was a born fighter. Gathering around a pot of stew was almost a weekly occurrence as Michael would enchant everyone with stories of how he bare-knuckle boxed two men at the same time and when he took on a guy who stood at nearly seven feet tall. One could make the case that he was perhaps exaggerating, as many good storytellers do but soon Charlie would get a glance of Michael in action.

Once, when Charlie was cutting through the field to get home from school he could hear shouts emanating from the nearby carriages that were scattered along the greenery. "Go on Michael. Use the elbow!", "Pin him down Rory, pin him down!" Charlie creeped over to get a better view. Both men were bare-chested with Michael's opponent sporting a large cut to the head where blood was gushing out over his stomach. Charlie was just in time to see the final blow be delivered as the baying crowd roared in delight.

Michael walked a couple of paces towards a small packet of cigarettes and lifted one out and placed the tip in his mouth. He then turned to his floored adversary and muttered through his lips "Now, these are mine now, do ya hear? I beat chu' for them fair and square." Charlie could scarcely believe what he had witnessed. A bloody brawl, all for a pack of cigarettes. Michael then spotted Charlie peering from behind one of the carriages. He pointed towards him and beckoned him over. "Come here young McNamee, I got a job for chu' and my boy Sean if you fancy it?" Charlie dared not decline his offer, he didn't want to risk upsetting the king of the gypsies. "Sure…what do you need?" Michael took a drag from his cigarette and blew smoke into the crisp evening air. "I'm heading into town to pick up some scrap metal to be sowl, could do with a couple of strapping lads to help me out." And so Michael, Sean and my Dad set off on the lowered seat attached to Michael's chestnut horse to make the winding trip into the hustle and bustle of local folk that Michael hoped would have some metal going spare.

2 hours later, after travelling from house to house along the pavilion looking for scraps, they managed to acquire several pipes, an old swing set and a few rusted out bikes. It was hardly a money making haul and they were on their way back with their loot tied up in the small back wagon when a short, bald man with a moustache and wearing an apron came rushing in front of the horse, startling the creature and causing Michael to rear up in surprise. "Whoa, Betsy, whoa!" he bellowed. "Good God man, you gave her a wile fright. You trying to get yourself killed?!" "Michael, Michael" the man panted breathlessly, "That bastard drunk Sam has only gone and robbed the charity tin from our fundraiser last night!" It turns out this stout man was called Danny, a bar man from a local pub who was a trusted friend of Michael's. "Now slow down, sonny" Michael replied, "How do you know it was him?" "He was the only punter sitting up at the front of the bar this morning, and the tin was resting on the table top but when I turned my back for a split second and then looked back around, him and the tin were gone."

Michael puffed out his cheeks, being the local go-to man was exhausting work. "Alright, I think I know where to find him, looks like we're going on a detour, lads". He shook the harness attached to Betsy and the three travelled for a few minutes into a decidedly more rustic part of town. Run-down shops that were boarded up and drunks on the street were the order of the day and surely enough Michael spotted the truant thief ducking into another establishment. "Right fellas, follow me" Michael instructed as he ushered Sean and Charlie into the bar. It didn't take long for Michael to clock onto this Sam character. He was an older man with squinted eyes and grey stubble across his face which was dewlapped with dirt. He wore a large mustard coloured over coat and raggedy workman's trousers with boots that had several holes in them.

He certainly didn't look like the kind of man that would be carrying swathes of cash, and Michael bounded across the pub as soon as he clocked him brandishing a £10 note. Michael was strong as an ox and lifted the shady figure off the ground by his collar as Sam whimpered like a little puppy being disciplined by its prudent master. Michael glared him in the eye and said through gritted teeth. "So where's a lowlife like you getting that kind of money from, eh?" Charlie glanced around at the sea of faces cowering behind their pints as they looked on with a mixture of curiosity and apprehension. "I've been working at the docks… lifting crates of fish and crab and stuff he spluttered, "Honest I have". "Oh, really?" Michael gave him another huge shake and sure enough the tin came rattling out from under the coat of Sam's. "And do they pay you in tins as well? You lowlife bastard!" He barked as he hoisted the bewildered figure onto a nearby table like a man in the scrapyard throwing a large pane of glass into the recycling bin. "You, sir, better get out of my sight before I do something you're not gonna like!".

The bumbling drunk then staggered off the table and onto his feet, and Sean and Charlie watched as he scuttled out the door and disappeared over the horizon. Michael lifted the tin off the ground and removed the notes within that were tied together by a rubber band. He handed the wad of notes over to the barkeep. "See to it, that this makes its way back to Danny's bar" He instructed. "And nobody go about helping themselves to a stash of the goods, cause I'll find out if some goes missing, ya hear?" Everyone in attendance nodded like a cascade of obedient schoolchildren towards their imperious headmaster. Charlie was in awe of this man. The respect he commanded with his presence was something else. Perhaps he was well deserving of his local accolade as King of the Gypsies.

Chapter 4
The uncles from hell

Unfortunately for Charlie those carefree days of sunshine, leisure and splendour were not to last. In order to help with the workload on the family farm, my dad was sent to live with seven of the most devious, despicable and brutish drunkards you are ever likely to meet. Their names were Frank, Thomas, Adam, Richard, Declan, Stuart and Paul. Instead of being like Homer the Greek author and affording these men long, lengthy descriptions of their appearance and character; I will simply summarise these cretins in a few sentences. They were scruffy, filthy, almost always drunk and downright cruel to my dad. They were figures that exploited everything for their own gain, including cheating their own sister; Charlie's Mum, out of her inheritance that she was due for the farm when it was being sold by tricking her into signing documents that jousted her out of any claim to the property.

So these were the scoundrels that my dad would have to spend the rest of his innocent youth with and they ran him ragged around the farm. He had to milk the cows, tend to the chickens, clean the stables and gather provisions from the local shop, many of these chores would have to be completed before he set off for school. One day when feeding the horses, one of his uncles strode into the stables. "Hey, boy- get yourself into the back of the wagon! You're helping us manage the greyhounds down at the dog track" and so Charlie clamoured into one of the backseats as his uncles squeezed in, nursing bottles of beer as they bumped down the road. "So who's for winning the race down by fisher's market at 3.20?" Richard bellowed. Charlie chirped up "I hear that Ferguson's dog *Lightning Streak* is a fast runner". The next thing Charlie knew he felt a sharp, warm smack from behind his ear. "No one's talking to you" Adam slurred. The ragtag band of brothers were already well on their way to being intoxicated as they kept bumping into one another like a bunch of bowling skittles as they rattled down the road with Charlie feeling the brunt impact of their wavering elbows as they swayed back and forth.

When they arrived at the races, Charlie was ordered to lead the first set of dogs into the kennels for the start of the races. After an afternoon of going back and forth with the dogs, tending to their needs and making sure they didn't get too riled up or have a go at biting one another, the dog handler would often throw Charlie a pound or two. This of course went straight into the pockets of whatever uncle would be first to nab him as he walked out from the starting track. To be used for gambling and of course: Drink. "Don't we give you food, shelter and a place to sleep?" They would rhyme off habitually. "You need to earn your upkeep, boy." Charlie didn't mind the constant chores, he was just happy to be out of the house and away from the prying eyes and flailing fists of his uncles'. When out working he would try and time his return to the house carefully. As the months passed, he was able to gauge when they would be merry as drunks and when they turned nasty and violent. Despite this, Charlie got at the very least a smack two or three times a day, either for not being quick enough with the groceries or for spilling too much of the milk from the heavy buckets he had to saunter around the farm with. Once, my dad was caught eating a hotdog on Good Friday; a holy day when one is not supposed to eat meat, by Frank. He called him a "disrespectful little shite" and gave Charlie a good pasting, despite of course himself not being an overly religious man, far from it.

The condition of the main house was like that of a pig's sty. Crockery and crumbs engulfed the central living area. The kitchen was littered with empty bottles, some smashed that Charlie had to be careful to tiptoe around when he came in during the evenings. There were tea stains over almost all of the furniture and Charlie could take pride in the fact that the farm was at least semi-maintained whilst his uncles lived in squalor. Though this was rarely good enough for the horrible huddle as they would find fault from almost anywhere. "You didn't clean that stable right." Smack! "You're late again with the butter." Thump! It was like living in a sort of hellish circus, one from which there was no escape from the benevolent ringmasters that oversaw everything and that were all too comfortable with lashing out with their whips. It wasn't enough that they made Charlie's home life a domestic nightmare, but they also denied him other opportunities, like the chance to compete internationally in the high jump to represent his school. They refused him permission to leave the country. I guess 'someone' had to milk the cows. Further down the line, they would not only spoil his sporting dreams but would go on to commit an act so heinous and reckless, that it would change the course of Charlie's future forever.

Chapter 5

Showdown at the school

The day started like any other. Charlie was up early to feed the chickens and fill buckets of water, he then cut through the adjacent field, waving to the travellers as he passed them. Stinker was waiting for him at the bottom of the field. Stinker was forever scheming ways to cheat folk out of a few pound, like the time he convinced Charlie to distract the local shopkeeper whilst he filled his pockets with sweets and sold them at discounted prices in the schoolyard, and today was no different. "Listen here, Mac" he said as he ushered Charlie over. "I got a tip off the boys down at the race course, there's a horse called 'Golden Girl' who is an outsider at 20-1, but Chrissy's Da says she's in top shape and has been wrongly placed as an outsider." Stinker then reached into his pocket and brandished a five pound note, "I borrowed this here from me Da, I say we bunk off school and sneak in a cheeky wee bet, I know a guy who'll place it for us in at the bookies."

Charlie wasn't entirely sure "Gosh, Stinker, won't your da beat the head of ye for nicking that money?" Stinker however, was unwavering in his belief that he had picked a winner. "He won't be mad Mac, he'll be ecstatic when we bring home the winnings, so are you in or not?" Despite his reservations. Charlie was never one to back out of such a lucrative coup. "OK, let's do it!" He replied. The duo then made their way down a long, windy beaten path and cut through the backs of some nearby houses, they then hopped over an old wooden fence which took them towards town. They then ventured through the busy street for about half a mile until they were just outside William Hill's bookies. "Right." Stinker panted.

He was a heavy set lad and ran out of breath quite easily, "Murphy said he'd meet us round the side, come on." The two made their way to the side of the building wear a tall figure was waiting for them in the shade. "Alright, Murphy?" Stinker quipped. "What's happening, lads?. I understand youse are looking to place a wee bet…" "You're darn right!" Interjected Stinker. "5 punts on Golden Girl at 20-1". "20-1?" Said an astonished Murphy as he reached out and took the fiver from Stinker. He was a tall, gangly figure who had his ears pierced and wore a brown shirt with the collar turned up and the sleeves rolled to the elbows. He sported some stubble but still looked relatively fresh-faced.

A packet of cigarettes bulged from his front shirt pocket and he kept a cigarette tucked neatly behind his ear. "You sure about this, boys?" He enquired as he pulled the ciggy from behind his ear, popping it in his mouth and lighting it. "5 pounds is good money. You might be flushing it down the drain." "I have boys on the inside" Stinker replied confidently like a wily gangster. "We'll split the winnings. 40 for me and Mac and 20 for yourself." Murphy rubbed his hands together. "No sweat." He mumbled as the cigarette dangled from his lips. "I'll stick her on now for ye."

The two parted company with Murphy and made their way towards the school. "We'll slip in unnoticed." Stinker whispered "They'll never know we were gone." They slid through the school gate and ran towards the back entrance. It seemed they had gotten away with it… until they ran straight into Miss Carlisle: a short, pudgy woman with a beaky nose and coffee stained, yellow teeth. She was lingering by the back door as the boys entered. "And what time do you call this?!" She shrieked in a shrill voice "To the headmaster's office… NOW!" Charlie and Stinker walked gingerly to the office of headmaster Davies and knocked weakly on the door, but still loud enough for him to hear. "Enter!" He bellowed. The two made their way into the room. It was a very tight knit room with a large shelf to the right that had a catalogue of books and Mr Davies' various diplomas and awards hung above the case.

There were two green chairs sat parallel to his desk and he glared through his bifocal spectacles at the two boys. "Sit!" The two slumped into their seats. "Liam McAuley and Charles McNamee! What on earth are you two playing at turning up this late?!". "We had to go the long way cause there were someone's cows out loose on the main road, sir" Stinker mumbled. "Ha!" Davies cackled "I've heard some excuses in my day but that tops the lot. So, you're a liar as well as a truant. It seems I'll make an example of you two." He stood up from his desk and moved towards a small cupboard that had glass paned doors. He reached in and pulled out a long, brown cane that was chipped and had various marks on it, no doubt a result of all the occasions it had been used to thwack disobedient children. "On your feet!" The two stood to their feet. "Hands!" The boys reluctantly removed their hands from their pockets and stretched them out. Mr Davies hoisted his cane high above his head and brought it down with a smack onto Stinker's hands.

He winced in pain. Next up was Charlie, who received the same treatment. Each boy got 10 hard whacks. Charlie's hands in particular were red and swollen right up to his fingertips. "Now get to class!" Charlie had to explain to his teacher how he could hardly grip a pencil because of his wounds and so was forced to sit facing the wall for the rest of the day as punishment. However, it was when he returned home to the farm that the true tragedy of this episode would be set in motion.

Golden Girl finished 4th in the big race, so there was no consolation to be found anywhere for the boys. Charlie grimaced as his fingers caressed the udder of one of the cows, it was impossible to complete his chores with his injury. He meandered into the house. His uncle Thomas stood up from his chair with a scowl and shouted towards him "What are you doing, boy?! There's no way you could have finished milking them cows!" Charlie looked down at his hands. "I can't grip the udders" he whimpered. "My hands are wrecked". Declan called out. "Let me see". Charlie held his hands towards Declan's face. "Who the fuck did that to ye?" "Principal." Charlie mumbled. "Right!" Declan yelled "Come on lads. It's time we paid this guy a visit". The seven of them rushed out the door, leaving Charlie behind. In hindsight he probably should have left with them, though I doubt he could have prevented what was going to happen next.

The rusty old wagon pulled up just outside the school gates. The 7 uncles leapt out and made their way towards the front entrance. Mr Davies came to meet them at the steps. "Well, gentlemen" he said calmly. "What can I do for you?" "You the principal?" Stuart snarled. "Indeed, I am" Davies replied.

"How can I hel-…" Before he could finish, Adam punched him square in the nose and he fell to the ground. Some of the staff; who were watching from the windows came running out from the school building and chased them off. Needless to say my Dad was immediately expelled from school, something he remained bitter about even in his latter years.

He told me how "some may think my uncles were simply sticking up for me, but I knew them better than that. All they cared about was that the farm work was done and didn't think for a second how their actions would affect me. It certainly turned my life into an uphill struggle as I had no qualifications, no references, and was essentially left in the lurch."

Chapter 6

A working man

So my Dad was left with 2 options; Stay in the hellhole with his uncles or get a job and get out of there. He was only 15 but around his parts there was no-one enforcing the 16+ law. Besides, my Dad's circumstances were pretty extenuating after his uncles battered the principal. So for Charlie the hunt was on. After several unsuccessful attempts at finding paid work, he came across a building site. He approached the site manager and more or less begged for a job as he was desperate. "You ever worked on a site before?" The grey-bearded man in a yellow hard hat and orange vest asked. "No, sir, but I've worked on a farm most of my life and I'm good with my hands." The manager looked him up and down. "Hmm." He muttered. "I might have something for you. I'll start you off in brickwork, minimum wage of course as you're only an apprentice.

You can pick up your hard hat, vest and trowel from the supply closet out back." Charlie was ecstatic "Thank you, Sir" He spluttered, grabbing the man's hand and shaking it vigorously. "You start tomorrow. 7am sharp." Charlie walked back to the farm with a skip in his step. It wasn't much, but he had taken the first step towards being free from his uncles once and for all. Now he needed a place to stay. Something cheap of course but anything was better than the smelly, beer- soaked pit that he was residing in currently. So he went to sleep with a smile on his face, eager to make an impression the next day.

Charlie woke shortly after 6am. After all, for the time being he still had the farm work to do. Once he completed his chores he ran for the bus at the bottom of the lane and once aboard he gazed out the window as the sun shone in at him. He reached the site in 15 minutes and got himself kitted out. As he wandered onto the site, a young fellow; Only looking a couple of years older than Charlie reached out his gloved hand. He had a friendly demeanour and a wide smile on his face. "Please to meet you, the name's Ben. First day doing brickwork?" "Yep" Charlie replied. "Ah, there's nothing to it, I'll show you the ropes." Ben then led Charlie further into the site yard.

After a slightly shaky and uneven start, Ben's guidance began to pay off and he soon got the hang of it. Ben seemed like a real nice guy, a solid all-round bloke and the two conversed as they ate lunch together. "So, where are your digs then?" Charlie swallowed a mouthful of his sandwich. "I live on a family farm up by Glendale Road, but I'm looking to move out..." "Oh funny that" Ben interjected. "My old housemate is moving out next week to go live with his fiancé in Glasgow. There's a spare bedroom there if you want it, and the rent's cheap too." Charlie nearly choked on his sandwich as he could barely contain his excitement. "Really?!" He asked, almost in disbelief. "That would be great!". "It's settled then." Chuckled Ben. You can move in as soon as Jack leaves next Wednesday." Charlie was beginning to think that maybe things were starting to look up after all.

The next week seemed to drag by for Charlie. He just couldn't wait to be free of those bullish arseholes he called uncles. He didn't even bother telling them he was leaving, till the night before. Declan called him an "Ungrateful wee shite." And as he was leaving a drunken Paul stood in the doorway "So that's it then?" He slurred "After all these years of feeding ye and giving ye a place to stay, you're just walking out on us. Ye dirty little fucker!" Charlie dropped his suitcase and clenched his fist. He didn't have to live in fear of his uncles anymore. It would have been easy to deck his uncle there and then. He was now big enough and strong enough to take on any one of the drunken buffoons but instead just nudged Paul out of the way. "I'll not be back." Charlie said with a smile. "So good luck running the farm without me. You pack of wankers!". He strode leisurely away from the house, but there was one more pleasant goodbye to make. He strutted into the stables and made his way to his favourite brown chestnut horse who he had watched grow up from a foal that he called Felicity. "Well, girl. This is goodbye, you're the only thing I'm going to miss about this place" He whispered. "So long, girl" He smiled as he stroked her one last time. He then picked up his suitcase and made his way to the ragged bus stop for what he hoped would be the final time.

Chapter 7

The 20 Pence Park Scandal

Charlie and Ben's little house was adjacent to the local primary school: St Bartholomew's. The fervent cheers of children could head from their kitchen window, and as the swathes of youngsters poured out into the school yard, their roars of joy engulfed the street. Charlie wasn't deterred by these noises; it beats the drunken jeers of his uncles any day of the week. On his way back from work, Charlie liked to cut through the local park. Despite the rustic nature of the surrounding street, the park was surprisingly well maintained. The swings were in immaculate condition, and the silver slide shimmered on a sunny afternoon. There were several trees that possessed an impressive cluster of leaves that arched over the park's pathway to provide a pleasant, cool shade. There were also long stretches of neatly cut grass, ideal for picnics or to just lay back and gaze at the sky. It was on his way through this park that Charlie noticed an odd gathering of silhouettes under the shade of one of the trees. There seemed to be a rustling amongst the shadows, and then a tall figure disappeared into the distance, leaving the two smaller silhouettes alone. Charlie at first thought nothing of it, probably just kids trading sweets or battling conkers. So he made his way on home.

He decided the next day to check and see if there were any more suspicious movements in the shadows and this time he noticed 4 silhouettes back this time, with 3 of them being considerably smaller than the other one. This piqued Charlie's interest. He waited in the brush until the tall figure departed and then stepped out in front of the smaller figures. "Well, guys, who was that you were talking to?" he asked with his hands on his hips. The three children exchanged nervous glances, and then one of the boys spoke up. "They were giving us money for sweets" he mumbled and holding out his hand, brandished two 10p coins. The freckled youngster who sported a short fringe and button nose kept his eyes fixed on the ground, as if he was bearing the burden of some great shame. "So just like that?" Charlie questioned "He just gave you money for sweets for free?" Again the kids looked around at each other nervously, "yep" they murmured, "just like that." Charlie wasn't convinced but nevertheless departed, although when he got back to the house he asked Ben "You notice anybody acting suspicious round the school or park?" Ben replied "Em, no not really. Some of the older kids like to smuggle cigarettes and beer down the back alley near the local primary. Why do you ask?" Charlie replied. "Just saw some tall figure lurking about the park, kids say he was giving away money for them to buy sweets. Something about it just doesn't sit right with me."

The next day was a Friday, and Charlie and Ben were able to leave work at an earlier time, shortly after lunch. The two men decided to head to the local convenience store to see if they could uncover any clues about this mystery money lender. They asked Mr. Garett, the conveyor of shop if he noticed anything unusual. "Well" He said, turning to face the men after storing away a large box of marshmallows and fudge. "I have noticed that there aren't many kids about immediately after school, but about an hour or so later they seem to flock in with money to spend. I just assumed they got it from their parents." Ben checked his watch. "Another hour and fifteen minutes till the kids get out from school. I say we come back in the evening and see if our man shows up."

So, they made their way to the park later that day and towards the secluded space under the trees. They stayed out of sight and soon enough the tall figure showed up again. There appeared to be some conversing, a little giggling, and then the figures departed. Charlie waited till the figure had walked out of sight before leaping out, and with both hands, grabbed the man by the collar and flung him sharply against a brick wall in one swift movement. "Right, mucker," he seethed. "You better start talking and talking quick. What were you doing with those kids back there?!" The man's face was aghast with terror as he spluttered his response. "It's just money for my nephew, money for sweets. Honest, I swear!" Ben chirped up. "You must have a lot of nephews then, because that crowd of kids is getting bigger by the day." "They're just his friends" the man replied, "just his buddies!". Charlie loosened his grip slightly, but his icy glare remained intact. "Say he is your nephew, why not just go into the shops with him and his friends, why exchange money in the dark. Away from everyone?" The man paused for a second, almost as if to gather his thoughts. "My sister doesn't let me see him. We had a big fight and so all of our meetings have to be in secret…" Charlie let the man go, and as he regained his composure Charlie still hovered around him in an uncomfortable proximity. "Get out of here, and if I find out you've been lying. I'm coming for you." The man backed away. He was quite tall, and really skinny. He wore a brown, buttoned up jacket and his gangly arms hung down by his side, he also had some stubble on his chin and a weedy moustache that looked more like whiskers than anything else. As he sauntered away, a little girl in pigtails and pink dungarees came skipping merrily around the corner. "There he is!", She cheered, pointing in the direction of the skulking figure. "There's the man who gives us money for tickles!"

Tickles?!

Charlie and Ben glanced at each other and then back towards the tall figure who upon hearing the girl's statement took off like a rocket through the back pathway of the park and hurtled over a nearby gate. Charlie and Ben set off and were in hot pursuit, panting heavily as they charged through the bushes and bounded over a small wall that sat opposite the football pitch. The man then ran through the back yard of Mrs Trilly's and trundled on through the graveyard that was just inches from the house. Here was where the tall man made his escape as he mounted a nearby bicycle lying pressed up by a tiny workman's shed near the graveyard entrance and sped off down the road. It was all downhill from there and so the two men had no chance of catching the pervert now. "Fuck!" Charlie shouted as he regained his breath. "The bastard got away!" Ben then said "I just hope that's the last we see of him near any children." The two made their way back through the graveyard towards the park and by the shop before returning home as the evening glow of the sun disappeared behind the clouds.

A few weeks later the mysterious park paedophile found his way into the local papers. It was revealed that the man's name was John Hanasen. He was a 43 year old who became a highly sought after figure after kids started reporting to their parents how he gave out 10 and 20 pence pieces to coerce the children into taking off their jackets and coats so he could 'tickle' them. He was eventually arrested after a local discovered his badly bruised and beaten body by the hedges near a busy road, most likely the handiwork of a vigilante or several of them. "Good enough for the bastard!" Ben nodded as he set down the newspaper flat in front of himself on the kitchen table. "It looks as if there's some justice in this messed up world after all."

Chapter 8

Birth of the Siontists

It was a cool, crisp Autumn evening, and Charlie and Ben decided to call into the local pub: 'The Duck & The Hound' for an evening tipple. They had just spent their Sunday placing a few bets down at the racetrack. Charlie's enthusiasm for watching the dogs had not diminished in any way even though it was the site where his uncles could be guaranteed to rear their ugly heads, and brought back memories of the verbal attacks they would took so much pleasure on unleashing his way whenever he did something wrong, or if they lost a bet which gave them another excuse to abuse in some way the young boy. However, Charlie, as much as he would like to teach the lowlifes a lesson, refrained from taking any decisive action. He would keep to himself as long as it was reciprocated, and his uncles would know better now to challenge a grown man who was in every way inclined to give them a pasting if he so desired.

The Duck and the Hound was a quaint, cosy little bar that sat opposite a creagh concrete factory site. Naturally, given its location, it was a popular venue for the working men, who loved to stream in for a late afternoon pint after they were off duty. This being the weekend, however there was a greater variety of personnel that visited the establishment on this day. There were a group of young men and women sat in the booth that directly faced the fireplace that you could warm yourself by as you turned left past the entrance. Above the fireplace, there was a deer's head whose antlers protruded in dramatic fashion up towards the roof of the building. Whether it was real or not, nobody thought to ask. This wasn't a place for questions, or any inquisitive behaviours. The string of older locals who were propped up around the bar glared with a scowl as the two men entered and sat on a small round table facing the makeshift stage which was set up quickly and consisted of a makeshift platform of rectangular wooden boxes and a few stools set up around the stage's perimeter. There was a single microphone placed close to the stage's precipice and a young, tanned face fellow with long blonde hair that was slicked back swaggered onto the stage, closely followed by three accomplices. The blonde-haired lad had an acoustic guitar that hung round his neck, one of the other lads also wielded a guitar of the same fashion. The third one had a bass guitar, and the final member had a small set of drums that he kept adjusting as they threatened to fall apart on the sporadically shaped stage.

The blonde lead singer greeted everyone with a grin as he took his place at the stage front, as if he was trying to infuse some of his own positivity onto the watching audience who were in no mood to return his gaze with any similar etiquette. "Bloody waste of time" grumbled one of the regulars. "What's the craic with this lot, barkeep?" Another said and gestured towards the bar man and then the stage with a bony, wagging finger. "A pub is a place for a drink and a chat, not to listen a lot of this nonsense by a bunch of posers!" Nevertheless, the young lad spoke into the microphone with clarity and confidence. "Well hello to all the folks in Sion, my name is Terry and these are the sky-blue swingers, closing off our tour of the glens before heading off to England to try our hand across the water…". "And good bloody riddance!" yelled an old man at the back which was greeted with a large cheer. The young man cleared his throat and turned towards the rest of the band. "All right lads, let's give these old fogies a show… and a one, two, a one, two, three four…" and the band bounced into life. Charlie had always been a fan of live music and was mesmerised by how elegantly but also powerfully the lead man strummed his guitar and belted out the vocals, all to the rhythm of his band behind him…

#Well down the road on a summer's day a girl I did meet#

She was rough and ready, hot and heavy, and I swept her off her feet#

Now the band does play and the people sway, here right now every night and day#

She stole my heart, and that was just the start for my own little country beau#

Ben glanced around him and noticed the brows of the regulars began to soften a little. He then turned back to Charlie, "Hi, these lads aren't half bad ye know? Even with a tough crowd an all." Charlie then leaned over, with his eyes still fixated on the band's frontman. "Wouldn't it be great to master an instrument like that. To be able to influence a crowd with such power?" "Not to mention the ladies go mad for it!" replied Ben "I know there are none here tonight but do you ever see that man Mick Jagger? Barely sings or so much as roars into the microphone and a quick shake of the hips and the ladies fall at his feet. Same with that guy in America, Elvis too." The two listened intently as the men played out their set for the night, and as they rounded off and began to pack their gear away, Charlie and Ben approached the lead singer. Ben being the more forward and confident of the two perked up. "Nice gig, lads. Was a cracking show". The front man Terry removed the guitar from his neck and held his hand out to shake with a big grin. "Cheers, fellas" He said warmly. "Always nice to hear folk say they enjoyed the session." Ben then took a step closer and pointed towards Terry's acoustic guitar. "Where might one go about getting themselves an instrument like that?" He said slapping Charlie on the back. "Me and the young fella here were thinking of starting our own little circuit. Ye know. For a bit of craic?" "Well", said Terry as he lifted the guitar and held it out towards Charlie "This little baby has been with me for some time, she'd be worth close to 80 or 90 pounds on the market." Ben's face visibly sunk "Oh." He murmured "Bit out of our price range that". Terry took another glance at the guitar, then back at Ben and Charlie and smiled. "Tell you what, this label in England are giving us all our own brand new equipment, provided for and paid for by our sponsors. I'll give you this for thirty pounds. You'll not get a better deal than that." Ben turned towards Charlie. "How much money ye got left?" Charlie pulled out a fiver and some pound coins. "Just under a tenner... not even close." "Well I'll stake the rest of it for you, call it an investment. You can pay me back once we're sweeping the country and packing out all the bars across the region" Ben grinned. Charlie chuckled and shook his hand "Yeah, sure thing." The three men made their transaction and parted ways. "Soon that'll be us Mac. We'll be getting all the big gigs across the country and beyond. Just you wait and see." Charlie swung the guitar around his neck and played a few chords. "It's been a while since I last played, probably a bit rusty." He strummed a few chords again "So what are you going to do then?" he queried at Ben "Me? I'm going to sing of course. I'm not the best but damn it I'll put on a good show!" The two men flopped down on a park bench, the evening darkness had swept across the land now, and the gentle chirping of birds could be heard as well as the rustling of shops closing and punters leaving establishments as they made their way onto the town square. "So what we gonna call ourselves then?" Charlie asked as he inspected the fine craftsmanship of his newly acquired instrument. "Well, we're both from Sion Mills, so that would make us the two lads from Sion, perhaps they'll call us, the 'Siontists.'

"The Siontists?" Charlie pondered. "Yeah, it's got a decent ring to it. The Siontists from Strabane."

"I'm telling ye, Mac", Ben remarked, "This is the beginning of something special. I can feel it. Just you wait and see."

Chapter 9

Ways of the guitar

Within the four walls of their cottage; Charlie and Ben were sat facing each other on two wooden chairs as a couple of mugs of tea were situated at the men's feet. Charlie played a few more chords and Ben tapped his legs as if attempting to guide the beats in a rhythmic fashion. Charlie then stopped abruptly and removed the guitar from around his shoulder and allowed it to fall to the ground as he groaned in frustration. "It's fucking hopeless! I'll never get the hang of this song by tomorrow night." Ben and himself had managed to broker a night in a rustic pub for their first gig. They would be paid a twenty each and would be allowed a complimentary drink at the bar. "You'll get the hang of it mac" Ben said reassuringly. "Now once more from the top, and a 1,2, a 1, 2 ,3,4". Ben threw his head back and sang loudly.

#There was a sweet young filly who hailed from Duncrilly-

#With eyes as blue as the sea

And no matter how hard I try-

#I keep glancing as she passes by and I knew she was the one for me…

Charlie then plucked another bum chord and yelled in frustration. "I can't do this! My bloody fingers aren't doing what my brain wants them to." Ever the optimist, Ben smiled in reply. "Come on. I think we've earned a break. Let's go for a walk and clear our heads."

The two departed from the cottage and ambled down the street. The sky had a pleasing hue of orange and blue as the sun began to set behind the clouds. The two men were still learning new things about each other and exchanged tales of childhood, locations they were fond of and cherished memories as well as stories about folk they weren't so fond of.

Charlie could fill a book about folk he wasn't very fond of. They stopped outside a tiny one room café and had two strong cups of black coffee, hoping that the rich, bold flavours might ignite some spark in their brains that would turn them into accomplished musicians. They were sat for about 15 minutes when 3 girls approached their table. One was wearing a purple vest top with tattered jeans, she had blonde hair and a pierced nose. The girl stood in the middle of the trio had short, chestnut hair that just reached her ears, and sported a black and yellow overcoat. The third had a long bag strapped over one of their shoulders and was chewing gum loudly as she eyed the two lads up and down.

The blonde-haired girl leaned over the small table and it groaned under her weight. How embarrassing Charlie thought, would it be if the table should collapse and leave the lady in a heap on the floor. Nevertheless, she persisted. "The name's Charlotte" she then swung her arm behind her dramatically and pointed at the other two. "This is Bianca, and this is Eilish. We're having a bit of a knees-up for my sister Rebecca's 18th and we're looking for some live music for tomorrow afternoon. We spotted you with a guitar strapped around your shoulder the other night outside of Fitzy's place."

Charlotte then tapped Charlie on his arm and just let her fingers linger for a moment on his shoulder whilst the other two girls glanced at each other and giggled. "So, are youse up for it then?" Ben and Charlie were hesitant to respond. They weren't accustomed to such forward displays of female attention and were a bit taken aback by the confidence of the troupe. "Sure…why not?" Ben eventually stammered in reply. "Where will we meet you?" "Our address is 12 Salsbury drive" Charlotte chirped. "Be there around 5.00… see ya later boys" she trilled and the three departed. Once they had disappeared out of sight, Charlie turned on his companion. "What the hell were you thinking?!" he barked. "Agreeing to that, sure we can barely strum out a tune between us. We'll be the laughing stock of the town!" Ben sat back and smirked. "Chill mac chill. This will be perfect practice before our gig at the pub tomorrow night. And besides, all bands need a few groupies for their image" He chortled as he smacked Charlie playfully on the arm that Charlotte had been directing so much attention towards. "We impress the girls, then head to the evening session and put on a good show. The wheels are in motion now, Mac. So come on, back to the house and let's get practicing!".

Later that evening Charlie and Ben arrived at the front door of a small semi-detached house. The walls of the house were white and gritty and were stained with a black substance a bit like oil. The door was a mixture of brown and grey and had a Victorian style knocker. The boys took a glance at their surroundings. Two houses down and to the right was a cemetery and directly adjacent to it was the local church. It was a particularly foggy afternoon which added to the eerie mystique of the street. Ben took the initiative to bang on the door. Charlie stood behind him, tapping his feet with his guitar slung over his left shoulder. As if he was preparing for his showcase performance by discovering the rhythm within him. A few seconds passed and Charlotte answered the door.

The boys inhaled a waft of strong-smelling perfume as this blonde beauty stood before them in the doorway. Unlike their previous encounter, when she had her hair up in a bun, it was now draped down over her shoulders. She wore a long flowing green dress and purple high heels, her eyes were made up with black eye liner and her lips were ruby red. The two lads were half entranced as she greeted them. "Hiya, boys" she cooed. "Glad you could make it. Everyone's gathered in the kitchen, let me introduce you to the gang". She took Ben by the arm and Charlie sauntered behind them as they made their way into a brightly lit room that had a banner and colourful ballons dispersed throughout as well as a considerable amount of alcohol in cases and bottles that lay spread out on aa large table. "Everybody", Charlotte called out. "This is Ben and Charlie, they're going to play for us tonight!". A loud cheer erupted amongst the small but boisterous crowd as they raised their cans to toast the two gentlemen.

The birthday girl Rebecca approached the lads and pointed them towards the bounty of booze. "Help yourself to a drink or two" she pointed out. "Settle your nerves before you play.". "Nerves?!" Ben chuckled. "We don't get nervous do we, Mac?" he said as he slapped Charlie playfully on the back. "No, not at all" Charlie mumbled in replay in a considerably less confident manner. An hour or so past and the crowd became eager to hear the boys play. Charlie limited himself to only two drinks so as not to impair his quality of playing for his debut performance. Charlie tuned his guitar, and the crowd began to gather in a huddle to witness the first gig of the Siontists.

Ben stood up beside Charlie and waved to everyone as he introduced himself. "Hi, y'all, my name is Ben and this is Charlie Mac and we are the Siontists of Sion Mills…now a 1, 2, a 1, 2, 3, 4" he bellowed as Charlie strummed along and nodded in rhythm

"#So I came across a young girl, she went by the name of Jamie-Lee.

#I vowed to take her by hand and wanted to set her free.

#But her brothers said as they stood in my stead that there's no chance she will come with me.

#They laid waste to my plan, she needed a boy not a man and so I never got to make her my Jamie- Lee.#"

The crowd clapped and whooped as the boys played on and they were met with cheers as they finished their set. The lads were then gathering themselves when they were approached by a tall figure wearing a long caramel overcoat. He was a particularly distinctive man to look at due to the fact that he had an eye patch over his right eye and a stump in place of his missing left hand. Throughout the festivities he pretty much kept to himself and came across as rather shy. Nevertheless, he decided to introduce himself to the band. "Hello" he uttered. "My name's Pete, I'm Eilish's older brother. I have to say, you boys put on a good show. You know I dabble in music myself, I'm pretty decent behind a keyboard, or at least I was before the accident".

He looked down towards his stump and the three were suspended for a moment in a kind of awkward silence before Ben broke the air of discomfort. "Well, thanks very much." He said cheerily. "Ye know we're playing down at the Duck & the Hound later on if you fancy coming along". There seemed to be glint in the eye of this tall figure and he couldn't help but allow a wide grin to spread across his face. "OK, sure, I'll be there" he said with an added sense of enthusiasm. The boys then said their goodbyes but didn't leave before Charlotte planted a kiss on each of their cheek's which made Charlie blush and left Ben grinning like a cheshire cat. As Ben walked out the door he shouted over his shoulder. "See ya tonight, Pete!" As Charlie was leaving he heard Eilish turn towards her brother. "Are you sure that's a good idea? Remember the last time you went to that pub, the hassle you got?" Pete then replied determinedly

"I can't hide away forever. It's time I took control and started living my life."
"OK", Eilish conceded. "But you be careful and if any trouble breaks out, you stay well clear" She said as she finished her lecture.

Chapter 10

In defence of a friend

Charlie and Ben arrived early to get a scope of the kind of audience they would be expecting at the Duck & The Hound. "We'll have our work cut out for tonight I think" said an uncertain Charlie, "the folk in here are more of the down and dirty drinkers, not a receptive audience of eager teenagers." Ben, being ever the optimist was feeling perky about the set they were about to perform. "It'll all work out Mac. Once we get into our rhythm they'll be clamouring to hear more." "I hope so" replied Charlie "Cos if they don't we'll be chased out of the bar and won't be able to show our faces round these parts for God knows how long!" As they finished conversing, the bar manager stepped forward to greet the two. "Well lads. Nearly ready to go?" asked the short and stout figure with a long protruding grey moustache and white sideburns. "Been a while since we had a live band in. Best of luck fellas" he chuckled as he stepped down from the makeshift stage.

The décor of the bar itself was typical of that in a predominantly nationalist/republican region. A green and white scarf hung high above the bar with a Glasgow Celtic emblem alongside it. A poster emblazoned with the slogan 'You are now entering free Derry' also stood tall with the infamous Tricolour flag covering the surrounding walls. "Oh look" Ben chimed in. "There's Pete. Hiya Pete" he waved as the gangly frame of their newfound friend ambled into the bar with considerable apprehension, like a fawn daring to venture into a new area of woodland, away from the caring clutch and protective gaze of their mother. As the two finished setting up, one of the regulars; a man in his forties who was wearing a large hoodie covered in white paint shouted over to the bar manager. "Hey Paddy, where did you gather this lot from?" "They're a newly formed group" he replied. "This is their first gig so go easy on the boys would ye?" "Oh, don't worry" the man smirked "We'll give them a decent reception won't we lads?" His question was met with a chorus of cheers from the booth at the back where 5 jovial drinkers had positioned themselves.

The rest of the bar was made up of some bystanders, and a few that were huddled around the fireplace. There was not a woman in sight, in fact, a good portion of the chat among the regulars consisted of them bemoaning their long-term girlfriends or wives. This bar was a safe haven for the men of the town to express their feelings in whatever way they so pleased. A dangerous allowance no doubt, for anyone who should rock the boat so to speak and disrupt the status quo.

Pete was not among the merry revellers but sat himself down on a stool at the end of the bar nearby the pool table. His eyes seemed to dart back and forth, almost as if he was waiting for something to kick off. Charlie finished tuning his guitar and Ben stood up beside the sole microphone. He smacked his lips to gain some moisture and so he could speak with clarity. "Good evening ladies and gentlemen…" "There's no ladies here, son" one of the crowd shouted which was met with a roar of laughter. Ben chuckled and was unperturbed and resumed. "I'm Ben and the fella beside me is Charlie Mac and we are the Siontists of Sion Mills!" He gave Charlie a quick nod and the guitar he wielded boomed into life as he strummed with passion and precision and Ben nodded along before counting himself in.

Their set lasted roughly an hour and the songs they sang included some covers as well as an original song they came up with called. 'The Flower of Sweet Strabane.' When they had finished they were met with a sparse applause, not exactly earth-shattering but decent for a start. Ben turned to Charlie. "Not bad for an opening night hey, Mac?" "Aye, no major fuck-ups so I'm happy enough" Charlie replied as he wiped the sweat from his forehead. Paddy approached the duo with a note in each hand. "There you go boys, that's twenty pound each, and help yourselves to a pint" he chortled as he gave the lads a glancing wink before departing behind the bar, "We best head over to Pete" Charlie suggested. "The fella hasn't moved from that spot all night."

The two meandered their way through the crown and sat themselves down beside their compatriot. "Well, what did ya think?" Ben asked happily. "Very good" Pete replied swiftly. "Enjoyed it a lot. So, are we heading on then?" "Whoa, what's the rush?" Charlie interjected. "There's a few pints of Guinness up there with my name on them. Come on, I'll get the drinks in!" "Well, okay" Pete replied softly. "I'm not much of a drinker but I'm sure one won't do any harm."

The evening ticked along as the lads sat and chatted whilst getting to know each other's backgrounds. It turned out that Pete used to play keyboards in a local group that were called 'Natural Instinct'. As the minutes passed Charlie and Ben ingratiated themselves with Pete to such a degree that he felt confident about telling them how he lost his arm and one of his eyes. It occurred when he was working on a building site where he was helping to construct office spaces for a company that made shoes. One of the structures collapsed and it fell, along with a number of bricks on top of poor Pete, with one of the bricks shattering the glasses he was wearing (this being a time with limited safety protocols) and the eye was left irreversibly damaged. The duo listened intently and thanked Pete for being brave enough to share his story. Pete, too felt better afterwards, this being a rare outing for him, and he was glad to be amongst friends.

The three got ready to move on out when a shout emitted from the other side of the bar. "Oi! Pete! Is that you?" A fellow with long blonde hair bounded his way across to the lads. "Oh, it's you Brad", Pete said meekly. "How are things?" Ben and Charlie eyed up the drunken figure. He was quite tall but not as tall as Pete. He had a cigarette placed behind his ear and was wearing a grey shirt that was besmirched with some sort of liquid. He then began to chuckle in a manner that seemed to make Pete uncomfortable. "Well, well" he announced. "If it isn't Pirate Pete!" Pete was noticeably agitated by this remark and his annoyance was reflected in his response. "I've told you Brad, I don't appreciate you calling me that." The boorish chap leant on a nearby stool and nearly lost his balance. He was clearly intoxicated and his speech was slurred as he continued. "Oh come off it Pete, I'm just having a bit of fun. I see your sister's not about, tidy little piece she is" he blurted out as he rolled his tongue in a repulsive manner.

Pete then stepped forward and displayed an uncharacteristic surge of rage as he stood face to face with his rival. "You leave her out of this you hear?" he announced boldly. Brad then leant forward "Or what?" he smirked. "Or you'll have us to deal with" chimed in Charlie. "That's right" Ben also interjected. "You're out of line here, pal". "Now now" croaked Brad in a typically hoarse tone. "3 vs 1 is hardly fair." He swirled round on the spot and shouted in the direction of the back booth. "Les, Tony! Get over here." Two burly chaps wearing green overalls ambled forward with their arms folded. They nodded in the direction of Brad and Brad grinned as his yellow, tobacco stained teeth were reflected under the bar's dwindling light. "We'll take this outside then, and you know what? I'll close one eye and tie one arm behind my back" he cackled. "Then maybe you'll have half a chance." His cronies accompanied him in laughing at Pete's expense. All the while, Charlie was standing with his fist clenched. He had grown up with drunken bullies and didn't have much time for low lives that preyed on the vulnerable. Something inside of him just snapped and he gently eased Pete aside before planting a headbutt right into the solar plexus of Brad who tumbled to the ground like a bag if spuds. In the next few moments all hell broke loose.

The hulking figure of Les lifted Charlie by the collar and in one swift movement, hurled him across the bar and he smacked into the back wall. His companion Tony picked up one of the snooker cues and pointed towards Pete. "You're next, you half constructed fucker!". Pete however was on his toes and was able to duck out of the way of Tony's swing. Ben darted his eyes back and forth, not quite sure what to do and in a moment of blind panic reached for a nearby lamp and brought it down on the back of Les' head, who then crumpled to the floor. Tony closed in for another swing at Pete who was scrambling to regain his feet recoiled in fear of the next fateful blow. Just as Tony was set to strike, a woman's shout could be heard from the entrance. "Leave him alone!" It was Eilish. "You lay a finger on him and my Da and his mates will be down here in a flash to sort youse out." Tony glanced behind him and dropped the cue. "Ah, he's not even worth the trouble." he mumbled and left out the back exit. However, Brad and Les were getting to their feet and still had looks of rage painted across their faces. "Go, go!" cried Eilish and the four of them fled from the pub. Thankfully, the two aggressors were too drunk and too heavy to chase them very far.

Once the four got to the bottom of the road, Eilish turned and clipped Pete behind the ear. "What did I tell you about mixing in with that crowd?! God dammit Pete!" Pete was quick to snap back. "It wasn't my fault. It was that fucker Bradley, you know he's bad news." "It's true" interjected Ben. "We were minding our own business and he started running his mouth off." "Well," said Eilish, in a much softer tone. "At least he had you two looking out for him. Thanks." She turned away and began walking in the direction of home. "Guess we should be heading back to the gaff" Ben suggested. He and Charlie shook Pete's hand. "Been a pleasure, Pete" Charlie quipped. "Hopefully see you around these parts and in less scruffy circumstances." Pete let out a chuckle. "That's dead on." He then turned and ran to catch up with his sister. "Guess we'll not be playing back at the Duck & Hound anytime soon" quipped Ben "Ah, who cares" replied Charlie. "The place was full of divys. Hopefully we'll be entertaining bigger and more receptive audiences in the near future."

Chapter 11

The big contest and Ben's distraction

With the unpleasantness involving the Duck & the Hound put firmly behind them, the two were on track for a big band competition. They pulled up outside a building called 'The Scenic Inn' where there was a large cluster of individuals carrying instruments. The whole site resembled that of a Woodstock gig where some were tuning their guitars, others were laid spread out on the small piece of greenery, taking heavy puffs from their cigarettes as the clouds of smoke ballooned into the air. Others were dancing and jostling about in circles as they moved to the rhythm of the various beats being offered up by the different bands. Charlie and Ben made their way to the front desk just inside the central building. Waiting for them was a bald man with glasses and a furrowed brow who seemed to be scribbling some notes. He then asked the lads without looking up. "Name and place of origin." Ben chirped in. "We're called the Siontists and we hail from Sion Mills." The man handed the two a small bit of paper with the number 12 written on it. "That's the order youse go on. You two are act 12. Concert officially starts at 7pm." The two departed from the building and since they had quite a bit of free time on their hands, began mingling in with the other bands that were waiting around patiently, more often than not with a cigarette or beer in hand. One of the lads from a band called "The Timberwolves" approached Ben and Charlie, sporting a friendly demeanour and a beaming smile. His name was Josh, and with him were two girls wearing short multi-coloured skirts and high-heels. One of the girls had hoop ear-rings and long, flowing ginger hair. Her eyes were done up with a bold, black mascara and her lips were ruby red. The other girl was a brunette whose hair was sported in a tight fringe. Her eyes were a hue of hazel and a little black bag hung over her shoulder. Josh had an arm around each of their waists. "Hi ya fellas, this is Tiffany and Prim. "Short for Primrose" interjected the brunette. "We're heading to McCafferty's bar for a pre-show time knees up. Fancy joining us?". "Sure" said Ben without a hint of hesitation. Ben was easily captivated by a pretty face, or in this case, a fine figure to match as well. "It's settled then" said Josh "Let's be on our way."

The five of them made their way into the hustle and bustle of McCafferty's. The lads were led through the clouds of smoke and jeers of the bar's patrons by each of the girls. Tiffany had Charlie's hand, and Prim had Ben's. After a couple of pints had been merrily sunk, Tiffany glanced wearily around herself before delving into her little black bag and producing a plastic satchel which contained a white powder. No prizes for guessing what the substance was. She carefully poured the contents into the form of s small mound, and using a small razor, divided the contents into 5 symmetrical lines. "There you go, boys", she giggled. "One for you, and one for you" as she tapped Charlie and Ben on the chest. Josh and Prim wasted no time in snorting up the produce along with Tiffany. Josh threw his head back and let out a great sigh. "That's the real stuff there lads" he chortled, "Go on then, get it into ye".

Ben glanced nervously at Charlie and then at the three others. "Oh fuck it!" he shouted as he bent over and sniffed up his line. The three let out a loud cheer, Charlie however, had no intention of giving into the pressure. "Not for me thanks, I'll stick to the beer", he said with an air of authority. He then grabbed Ben by the shoulder, drew himself close to his ear and whispered, "Are you sure that was wise? What if it messes with your performance?" Ben chuckled heartily and responded by asking. "Do you think I've got a chance with Prim? I think she likes me ye know?" Charlie rolled his eyes and drew Ben in again once more. "So that's what all this is for? To impress some girl?!" Charlie could feel the anger well within him and he swivelled and barked at Ben. "Get your shit, we're leaving" Charlie then turned with a forced grin towards the revellers. "Well folks, thanks for your company but we gotta head, gotta get ready for the show" "No stay, stay, won't you stay?" called out Prim as she pouted her lips and leaned forward. This was enough to sway Ben. "I'll... I'll stay" he stammered. Come on Mac, the fun's just getting started." Charlie was indignant, "No. no we've got to go now!" but Ben was resolute in his determination to stay. "If you want to go on ahead that's fine, but I'm staying" he quipped. He broke away from Charlie's grip on his arm and sat back on the stool beside Tiffany and Prim. Charlie's face was aglow with rage. He turned and made his way back out of the side of the bar and was seething as he muttered to himself. "That useless Ben bastard, he'll do anything for a bit of skirt. Hanging with a bunch of drugees, he's going to get in bother over this. That I am sure of."

Time began to tick by as Charlie waited with a mixture of rage and apprehension bubbling away inside of him. An hour passed, then two, and Charlie could take no more. "Unbelievable" he muttered to himself. "Probably face down in a back alley somewhere". He flung his guitar over his shoulder and marched back towards McCafferty's. Upon entering the establishment he headed for the corner of the bar where they had been sitting but no-one was there. He approached the bar and leaning over it asked, "excuse me, bartender. You didn't happen to see two guys and two girls hanging about here recently?" The bartender leant forward and spoke to Charlie in a husky tone. "Yeah I seen 'em. Kicked them out too. They were causing all sorts of ruckus. Jumping on tables and tripping over my regulars. Think they've maybe headed towards The Fort Inn, which is a bar about a stone's throw from here."

Charlie thanked the man and made his way up the road, and as he approached the bar he spotted out of the corner of his eye, Josh and Tiffany out by the entrance, smoking. He approached them but on this occasion he had no time for frivolities or pleasantries. He asked Josh directly. "Right, where the fuck's Ben? We're supposed to play in just over an hour's time." The two high drunkards looked at each other and burst out laughing. "I'm glad this is all one big joke to you" quipped, Charlie, "But play time's over. Where is he?" "Fuck knows" perked up Josh. "Wherever Prim is, you can bet that old Benny boy won't be far behind." "It's quite cute really" added Tiffany as she took a drag from her cigarette. "He follows her around like a little lost puppy."

The two then erupted once more into laughter. "I don't have time for this" muttered Charlie as he made his way inside. He ran around the place like a madman, desperately calling out to Ben amongst the swarm of patrons. The bar was quite a considerable size and had some fancy paintings and murals that depicted scenes from the Battle of the Boyne where king William of Orange conquered the forces of the exiled King James II. There were some patrons who glanced at him peculiarly as he raced past these ornate works of art. He had no time for a history lesson. After about 15 minutes, he leant back by the toilets to consider his next course of action, when he heard a muffled plea emanating from the Ladies' restroom. "Would someone help me, please. I'm not a pervert. I'm stuck. Hello, somebody, anybody?" Charlie knew instantly that only Ben was capable of such a disjointed whinge.

Charlie made his way to one of the stalls and as he opened the door he saw a most surprising sight. "Oh, fuck me." He put his hand to his mouth to stop himself from bursting into laughter because there was Ben, clear as day, tied up to the toilet lid. His hands were strapped together. "What the hell happened here?" Charlie asked after composing himself. "She took everything, Mac. Thought we were coming down for a bit of fun and next thing you know she reaches into her purse, yanks out some cable ties and fastens up my hands. That's when she nicked my wallet. The bitch! I only had just over a tenner in there anyway so that harlot is welcome to it." "Well".

Charlie sighed as he untied his friend. "Let this be a lesson to you. Don't get involved with strangers, and don't get involved with drugs." "Oh pack it in, Mac", Ben chimed in. "You sound like the old nun who lived by my high school." "OK, fine.", added Charlie "Let's just forget about this ordeal and stay focused cause we're up shortly in the big contest." The two lads meandered their way through the bar and began sauntering up the street. "I'm sorry Mac, for before", a humble Ben conceded. "Should have listened to you, ye were right about the whole lot of them". "Never mind now", Charlie replied, "You're here now and that's all that matters."

The two lads were sat in the changing room, anxiously waiting for their name to be called. Ben was sat upright and kept fidgeting from side to side. Charlie noticed this and said "Geez, Ben. You're not that nervous are ye? We've played in front of more hostile crowds than this." "It's not nerves, Mac, bloody hell" replied Ben. "I think it's the fucking coke. Making me paranoid as hell." Suddenly, a woman's head peeked in from around the entrance. "Act 12; The Siontists, you're up." The two of them gathered themselves and made their way through the backstage area, being careful to avoid the numerous tripping hazards that were strewn in their path such as a donkey costume and a variety of footballs and basketballs, It was well seen that that they were playing in a multi-purpose hall.

They approached the velvet green curtains that ruffled lightly as they brushed against it. Charlie peeked his head out ever so slightly as act 11 rounded off their session. As the previous act disappeared towards stage right, it was time for the two Strabane lads to take to the stage. They emerged onto the centre of the stage as the four suspended lights shone down on them from above. Charlie could already feel the sweat beginning to drip from his brow as it glistened under the intense lighting. Ben nodded towards him for reassurance as he approached the microphone. "Hey, folks. I'm Ben, this is Charlie and we're the Siontists." He then belted out into the microphone. "A 1, 2, a 1, 2, 3, 4!" And so they played their hearts out, with fluidity and flair and Charlie even sneaked in a wee guitar solo as they shook the foundations of the stage with their raw dynamism and the audience loved it.

Once they had finished, the band was greeted with a wall of thunderous applause as they rounded off with 'The Eye of the Tiger" with Ben and Charlie alternating the singing between them; a difficult skill but they pulled it off, much to the crowd's delight. As they made their way off stage the two men were abundant with energy as the adrenaline of the occasion pulsated through their veins. Ben was ecstatic. "Crikey, Mac" he said with fervour "That was a hell of a show we put on, huh, what do ya think?" "Yeah it was good", Charlie chimed in as he wiped his head. "Can someone grab me a towel. I'm sweating like mad over here." One of the stage hands hurled him a towel as he wiped his hair vigorously. The two men then sat back and were in a reflective mood. They gazed up at the night and sat in silence for a while as the stars twinkled majestically, and the sky was radiant with a hue of red and orange. There were also clouds that acted as an elegant blanket that stooped around the horizon and the air brought about a few leaves as it delivered a gentle whisper. "Well, Mac", chirped Ben "Think we stand half a chance?" "God knows" was Charlie's reply. "But hey, we put on a damn good showing. Cheers" and the two men clinked their beer bottles as they contemplated what the future might hold for the two of them.

Chapter 12

Sayonara to the Siontists

As the evening's contest drew to a close, the bands all gathered together in a cacophony of smoke and beer swilling that crowded the entire hall. A short, stout little lady ambled up towards the microphone with an envelope in her hand. "Now, ladies and gentlemen, it is time to announce the top 3 bands." You could hear her fingers flipping through the paper as she held it up close to the microphone. "In third place… Sonic Youth". There was a small ripple of applause. "In second place… The Siontists" Charlie and Ben glanced at each other. "Not bad eh, Mac, not bad at all". "We did good" Charlie added "so 100 quid split two ways is a decent day's work I should think." "And the winners", the lady continued "who will receive a whopping £500 and a recording deal is… The Wet 'n' Wild Ones, congratulations". There was a high pitched shriek of delight that cascaded down through the gathered members of the winning band as they embraced each other and jumped about ecstatically. Although, obviously disappointed that they missed out on the grand prize.

The notoriety that second place in this prestigious competition brought them meant they were able to secure gigs up and down the country. Word was spreading like wildfire, that this band of two originally sheepish boys were packing out bars all across the isle. It then occurred, on one faithful night, playing at the Harbour Inn in Donegal that a life-changing proposition would be presented to one of our faithful guitar heroes. Ben and Charlie were just clambering down from their set when a man wearing a purple blazer, and sporting a black, slicked back ponytail approached and shook each of them heartedly by the hand. "Brilliant set tonigt, boys. Really impressive" he beamed with a broad smile. The name's Danny Ruscoe and I manage No Way Down" He turned towards Ben. "That's a cracking set of vocal chords you got there kid. So where's your manager? I would like very much, to have a word with him." Charlie and Ben were taken aback by this request and Charlie began to stammer before Ben intervened. "We don't have a manger. It's always just been me and Mac from the very beginning." "Wonderful!" Danny cried out with enthusiasm. "Then it's you I need to talk to." "I'll be at the bar if you need me" Charlie said. He knew Ben was the best out of the two in handling these sorts of things. He had the gift of the gab so to speak and so he thought best just to leave him to it.

20 minutes or so past until Ben eventually sauntered over with a glum expression on his face. "Well?" Charlie asked. "Does he want to represent us?" "No, he doesn't" Ben replied. "Ah well," Charlie piped up. "We'll find another way through to the big time." "But" Ben said with more than a hint of trepidation in his voice. "He wants me to join No Way Down as their frontman." Charlie paused for a moment as he could feel a lump, catching in his throat. "Well, um, " he said meekly "What did you say?" "I said no", Ben replied. "I said it's me and Mac or there's no deal". Charlie had to fight back the tears in his eyes and the tremor In his voice as he contemplate' what to say next. He stood up, and with a firm hand on Ben's shoulder, and managed to splutter out the words. "Listen to me, Ben. You've been a great band member and an even more wonderful friend who helped me when I was at my lowest. What right do I have to take away from you, a once in a lifetime opportunity like this? Now, you march back to that man and you tell him you accept his offer." "But Mac" Ben stammered as he began to get choked up. "What about you?" "I have to go down a different path, but hey, my time will come to live out my dreams, so now you have to follow yours. Grab onto it as tight as you can and never let go." The two hugged each other warmly as Charlie sent Ben on his way. "Go" he said with a wide grin. "Go and chase down your dream."

Back home in faithful Strabane, Ben was busy preparing to travel on tour with 'No Way Down' over to the isle of Scotland. Charlie wandered into Ben's room just as he was zipping up his prized guitar. "Well", said Charlie. "You've come a long way kid. Ben turned around and placed his hand on Charlie's shoulder. "We've came a long way, Mac. "Trust me", he continued. "There is an opportunity for you out there just waiting to be snatched. "Now" he said in a decidedly more perky tone. "How about a farewell pint, before I head off tomorrow?" "Sounds good" chimed in Charlie "First round's on you then Mr. Big Time" The night came and went, and was filled with merriment, cheer, and well-wishing from folk who had heard about Ben's big break. Now, the morning light appeared over the horizon. The sun shimmered on the pavements, and in through the cracks of Charlie and Ben's windows. A few droplets of rain from the night before drooped onto the window sill and clung to the leaves that swayed back and forth and as they were caressed by the gentle summer breeze. Birds could also be heard chirping their sweet melodies and were perched on the trees and on the roofs of houses all along the neighbourhood. Charlie and Ben were gathered around the kitchen table, and were reminiscing about some of the scrapes they got into in the past. "Remember that time you knocked over that massive guy's Guinness down at the bar near the quarry?" Ben asked. "How could I forget?" chuckled Charlie. "He had me by the throat and then you came steaming in and covered his eyes, you could barely get your arms around his giant head and we had to leg it!". "Ha, ha, yes. Now those were good times" reflected Ben.

Charlie took a gentle sip from his cup of tea and then turned towards Ben. "You make sure you write to me" he said assertively. "I want to know how everything goes for you in this big new chapter of your life." Ben smiled and replied, "I'll write as often as I can." They then spent the last hour enjoying their final breakfast together, and soon enough though, the time had come. The squeak of the small, rustic bus's wheels came shuddering down the street and parked outside the gate. The band's manager jumped out of the bus and gave a solid knock on the front door. From inside, Ben gathered the last of his things. "Well, this is it" Ben said in a tone full of sorrow. "Time to hit the road". He gave Charlie the warmest of hugs and Charlie could feel the lump in his throat welling up again but managed to regain his composure. "So long, kid. I know you'll smash it. Don't be a stranger now, you hear?". Ben gave him a gentle nod "Loud and clear, Mac. So long, old friend." He lifted his guitar case and his belongings and opened the front door. "There's my man!" beamed Danny Ruscoe. "Ready to hit the big time?" Ben gave one last glance at the old homestead that harboured so many fond memories and then said in reply. "Yeah, let's do it." He boarded the bus and Charlie waved him a final goodbye. The Siontists of Sion Mills were no more. So for Charlie, it was all about life after Ben. What would he do now on the music front? Guess it was time to fly solo, at least for the time being until this golden opportunity that he's so readily on the lookout for finally decides to rear its head.

Chapter 13

Discovered by the Playboys

No, it's not what you think. We're not talking about the mansion ran by Hugh Heffner filled with lingerie models dressed as bunnies. They were a small rock band that originated in Scotland and played in the UK. They toured Scotland, Ireland and occasionally England and Wales. It was a typical Saturday in the Duck & the Hound one week. Charlie had thrown together a ragtag group of lads he knew locally to form a small band. My Dad sang lead and played his guitar, Jeremy did bass, Diarmad was on keyboard and his little 13 year old brother Timothy was on drums. They weren't much to look at, and didn't sound powerful but my Dad was just grateful to be playing again. He had honed his craft well in his spare time. There wasn't much else to do about Strabane now that he lived on in his own and once he finished work on the building site. The manager of the Playboys, a man by the name of Charlie Friel was sitting quietly in the corner with his pint. He noticed how my Dad didn't even have to glance at his guitar head whilst performing and his tone had a deep, profound bass to it. Not as good as Elvis' 'thank you very much' but nonetheless the talent was there.

He approached Charlie when the set was finished for the night and extended his hand. "Charlie Friel's the name. I'm manager of a local group called the Playboys. Our bass player Shane is unavailable." It turns out Shane's brother was smuggling guns for the IRA. (Irish Republican Army) They were having tea one night when the RUC (Royal Ulster Constabulary) burst down their door and pinned them to their dinner table demanding to know where his brother was keeping them. Shane politely told them to

"Go fuck yourselves", so now they were both in custody. "Can you play bass?" He asked. "No" my Dad replied. "But Jeremy could show me. Hey, Jeremy!" A thin lad in a baggy blue hoodie ambled over. "How does the bass work?" "Piece of cake, Mac. Just make sure that you wrap your first and middle finger around the cords good and tight, given that they're thicker than acoustic strings. Maintain a good grip on the head of the guitar and pluck with some force and you're set." "Wonderful" chimed in Friel. "Here's what we'll do. I'll get your address and leave you the sheet music for 'The Parting Glass', it's a Celtic song. You get your buddy Jeremy to show you how to play and next Saturday I'll drop by and take you to our grounds and let you play with the boys. If we're all suitably impressed. You're in." "Sounds like a plan." My Dad said in response.

Here was a chance to get out of Strabane and out of that goddamn building site. Getting good paid work was virtually impossible at that time, given the fact that as soon as it was discovered you were a Catholic you were ousted. It happened with my Dad during his tenure as a builder. He was working part-time as an apprentice electrician and after a year he gained qualified status. About a week later he was handed what nowadays would be known as your P45 or metonym as it's regarded in British and Irish slang, indicating his time of employment with the firm was officially terminated. Protestants held most of the top managerial, professional, scientific and technical jobs.

Catholics were massively underrepresented in those positions and also in relatively well-paid areas like the security forces, and the metal and electrical trades. On the other hand they were over-represented in such notoriously low-paid occupations such as construction and personal services. Thus Catholics were more prone to unemployment than Protestants, and where they did have jobs, they were generally lower down the occupational scale. So Charlie was determined not to allow this opportunity to pass him by. He and Jeremy would meet up every day after work and practice for about 3 hours. Taking breaks for the odd ciggy and beer.

The day came and Friel picked up Charlie in his mini, basically a dark orange version of Mr. Bean's bloody banger. They drove through the streets of Strabane. As they drove by there were kids congregating on the streets. Girls were on their skipping ropes, the boys were booting about an old football. About 4 or 5 lads no older than 10 were hanging outside the local shop and giving the finger to two RUC officers that were stationed across the street, calling them 'black bastards' and saying how their Dads were going to find out where they lived and 'kick their heads in.' Now for those unfamiliar with the Troubles, 'black bastards' is not a racial slur. Loyalists who were affiliated with the monarchy would conduct regular marches through the streets to signify their allegiance to Britain. They sported black bowler hats and bright orange sashes. They were nicknamed "The black 'n' tans" or "Black bastards." Most Catholics automatically associated the police in Northern Ireland with Loyalism and viewed them as an extension of the occupying forces given the way they were known to discriminate against and interrogate Irish Catholics.

Friel and Charlie arrived at a small community hall and the three players had almost all the gear set up and ready to go. Friel performed the introductions. "Gentlemen, this man here is Charlie McNamee. He's going to be filling in for Shane." Charlie was introduced to the cohort. First there was Alfie. He played keyboards and did vocals too. He had a dark brown hair and a fringe that nearly shielded his eyes, and a Freddy Mercury-esque moustache. Then there was Fergus on drums. He was a chubby fella with bright pink cheeks. I think he had rosacea. He sported a bright green shirt with the sleeves rolled up. Then there was Tiernan. The pretty boy of the group. He was wearing a black leather jacket, tight-cut jeans and light brown boots.

He already had a cigarette in his mouth and muffled "Please to meet you" as he shook my Dad's hand. He played acoustic. Not as well as my Dad, Friel conceded before they arrived at the venue but by fuck he wasn't going to tell him that. He was a temperamental figure and the last thing he needed was to be 2 men down before their next show. "Right gentlemen, when you're ready."

Dad rarely got nervous, but did when he knew the stakes were high. He told me he downed a pint of Guinness before Friel picked him up to settle his nerves. Over the years he told me that he developed such a tolerance for the drink that he would swig an entire bottle of vodka before a gig and nobody would be able to decipher that he wasn't stone-cold sober. So up he went, and they played 'The Parting Glass'. He told me the performance wasn't perfect, far from it but at the end of the day he had never played with these lads before and he managed to keep pace with them. He never learned to read sheet music in his life. He did know the names of the chords and became so profound with the guitar that in his later years that if someone requested a song for him to play for a wedding in a week or so he would land in to me and go, "son, look up this here song on the computer." I'd go onto YouTube, he'd listen to it. Then he'd bring out the guitar and begin strumming. "Play it for me one more time there…OK, I think I've got it." The night before the gig he'd then request to hear it one last time just to make sure everything was in order. Ronan Keating's "This I Promise You" was the last one I can recall him rehearsing before he passed. So, they finished the song and Friel came up to my Dad and said. "Not bad Charlie boy. We're heading on a tour of some of the local pubs down South on Monday. Do you think you'd be ready to leave with us that morning?" My Dad quipped in. "I'd have all my shit gathered and be away with youse tomorrow if you wanted!".

Chapter 14

The Irish fighter pilot and Gaeltacht gibberish

My Dad was touring with the Playboys through the Gaeltacht. The Gaeltacht refers to the designated areas of Ireland where Irish is the primary spoken language and is actively promoted by local communities. These areas are mainly located around the Western Coast of Ireland, covering large parts of counties such as Donegal, Mayo, Galway and Kerry, as well as sections of Cork, Meath and Waterford.

The Gaeltacht is dedicated too preserving the Irish language and culture and although very few people in Ireland are fluent in the language these days, there are still small, rural communities, particularly in Galway where Irish is still people's first spoken language. When I was at Our Lady of Lourdes High School, those taking GCSE Irish would spend a week staying the quarters of a large farmhouse just outside Galway. It was known as an "unplugged week" where no technology was allowed.

Apart from of course to ring home to families at the end of each day, but the entire time they would have to try and interact with the locals in Irish. Going to market, making purchases and delivering instructions to workers etc. At St. Mary's teaching college in the Falls Road, Belfast where I did my English Lit. degree, there was an option for teachers to take the Irish Medium primary teaching option, qualifying them to teach in both English and in primary schools down South where parents wanted their kids to essentially keep the language of their ancestors alive. It was in a pub in Galway where The Playboys were performing a night-time gig. Most of the crowd were youngsters who conversed in English, but there were still a few old heads who were talking in the native language. Situated at small table near the centre of the bar were three gentlemen. The barman told Friel that they were members of the Irish Air Corps.

The Irish Air Corps were formed in the 1920s. When World War Two broke out they weren't exactly thrust into the action like you'd imagine out of some scene from Top Gun. There are no records of Air Corps planes engaging any belligerent aircraft, although dozens of escaped barrage balloons were shot down by them towards the end of the war. The bad winter of 1962/3 incentivised the acquisition of helicopters and during the Troubles they required additional reconnaissance resources.

In 1972 eight Reims-Cessna FR.172H joined the Air Corps to provide patrolling, aerial surveillance, and aerial communications. They were provided by the Americans and subsequently the Americans trained them in their usage. The most noticeable figure of the three at the table was the guy who when he stood up was at least 6"4 and jacked to the teeth. His name was Sgt. Peter Davis. Now, technically if you're carrying out reconnaissance missions to suss out potential terrorist plots by the IRA, you're employed by the British Army. Here he was fine but if this was discovered up north he would be very fortunate to leave the place with his knee caps intact. He had blonde hair and a razor tight trim. He also had a stare that could slice straight through you but the bar man knew him since he was a lad and said he was a lovely fella.

When the barman introduced the band to him he shook their hands, conversed for a while and basically said to them that his philosophy in life was simple. "Don't bother me or my pals when we don't want to be bothered and we won't bother you." Next to him was an African-American chap called Amo. He was a Corporal. His Dad was from County Monaghan and his Mum was from Ghana. Amo is African for "eagle." Quite ironic given the fact he worked in the Air Corps. The third lad was a young fellow, no older than about 19 or 20. His name was Private Phillip McBride, and he was from Leitrim. He said that Sgt Davis was like a second father to him. He always had his back and on this particular night he could have two pints of Guinness tops, it was a Saturday night after all. After they had made their introductions, the Playboys got set up and the night was underway. The folk of Galway loved their traditional Irish ballads and there was clapping and dancing and twirling amongst the locals.

The night was full of merriment and good cheer, apart from one rather sour incident involving our three army friends that was quickly resolved. Basically, two morons came strutting past their table. One of them coughed and under his breath muttered "no darkies welcome." Sgt Davis stood up, lifted him by the collar with one hand and launched him out the double doors. His mate then went give him a swift kick in the ribs but he caught his leg and with his right hand punched him square in the jaw, knocking out one of his teeth. As he crawled out the door, Davis sat back down and accidentally grazed his white shirt with his blood spattered knuckles. "Shit!" He exclaimed. "That'll be near impossible to get out." "Give it here." The bar-man shouted over. "My wife'll sort it out. In the mean-time you can borrow something of my son's. He's not as tall as you but he's a big fella so you'll be fine." Davis took off his shirt and handed it to the bar-man. My Dad said his body was something like you'd see in one of them Greek epics. Like Achilles when we watched Troy together back in 2004 or the first Hercules film he saw when he was about 8. He said 3 of the girls sitting at the bar nearly fainted.

The bar-man came back with a large green, woolly jumper and handed it to him. Problem solved. So the night carried on and unfortunately, in the last few years or so, and now particularly with the Playboys who were all heavy drinkers. My Dad drank excessively. They all got hammered and after the gig he ended up passing out in the closet whilst going to get back his jacket. Now this tight closet was located at the very corner of the pub, and none of the other members were wearing a jacket so when my dad went missing for about 15 minutes after 1am, they assumed he had hailed a cab and went back to the local hotel they were staying in, so they left.

The next morning my Dad woke up. His head was pounding and his mouth was as dry as the Sahara. He came stumbling out of the closet on Sunday morning and there were a few locals in, they all looked like farmers. Probably had been up since about 5am tending to their duties and were calling in for a quick pint. Now my Dad didn't know a word of Irish, and quite frankly nor do I. I did it from Yr 8 to Yr 10 at Our Lady of Lourdes and when given the decision to choose between it and French for GCSE.

The choice was simple. Cause to say words like 'garden' and 'toilet' in French was 'un jardin' and 'une toilette.'. Whereas to say something like 'wall' in Irish was fucking 'balla.' I do remember the principal at the time; Dr. O' Cuinneagan whose doctorate was in Irish language and actually left his role at OLOL do go and edit an Irish dictionary. Sounds exciting, right? Would take one of the Irish classes for our year every week. He asked me to answer some question and instead of saying a word like 'Pacnura' I stumbled and said 'pancake.' The whole class laughed and that was my nickname for the next month. Now he was an eccentric man and a firm disciplinarian but the school did flourish under his leadership and he was a funny man. He used to call my sister Rosie "the flower of sweet Strabane" because of where Dad was from.

My mate Ryan was a skilled amateur boxer in Ballymoney and nearly every time he passed him in the corridor he would put his fists up and go, 'I'll teach you a thing or two, son!" And dance around him. I have two very vivid memories of Dr. O' Cuinneagan. On one of our first weeks back there was busy traffic. With buses and cars taking pupils to and from schools like Loreto, St. Louis and Cross & Passion intersecting throughout the village. We didn't have a lollipop man or lady. He literally, in his suit and tie, with his tie flapping about in the wind stood dead centre in the middle of the road, halted an oncoming car with one hand, and beckoned us across the road with his other.

The other was at my Mum's wake. The English teacher Ms. Coyles gave me a hug outside my house and said "Dr. O' Cuinneagan wants to have a wee word with you." I walked into my kitchen and amongst the crowd he was standing in the corner reading from a small Irish poetry book. I approached him but he didn't see me. I stood next to him for like 10 seconds and was just like. "Should I say something here or let him finish?". So me and my Dad obviously new the basics "Conas atá tú inniu?" (How are you today?) "Ta me go maith" (I am good) Charlie heard the locals rambling on and thought he heard someone saying "go maith" but he was completely lost. He told me they might as well have been speaking Hebrew. Thankfully, the barman's son was working that morning and he filled my Dad in, saying the band hung around for a while but assumed he left after they couldn't find him.

My Dad sat with his head pounding at the bar to try and decipher what to do next. He couldn't remember for the life of him where the hotel was, or what it was called for that matter. And obviously, no mobiles, so he was stuck. As he was gathering his thoughts, the Sergeant from last night came in. "Hi" he said the bar boy. "I had a bit of a spillage on my shirt last night and the barman said he would get it cleaned for me." "No problem" replied the boy. He fetched him his shirt. "Thanks" He then recognised my Dad. "You're the bass player from last night?" "Sure am", my Dad replied. "Where's the rest of your band?" "Long story short, I got left behind. They're at a local hotel but I can't remember what it's called.". Davis paused for a second. "Amo and I are staying at Phillip's before we return to base tomorrow. Come with me and I'm sure he'll get you sorted." "Cheers." So Dad travelled with the Seargeant to Phillip's small flat.

When they went in Phillip was listening to the Leitrim vs Sligo football match on the radio whilst Amos was frying up a few steaks with mushrooms, the sound of them sizzling in the pan was tantalising and the smell wafting in his direction had him salivating. "Christ!" Dad exclaimed. "You boys eat like this for breakfast every day?" "Breakfast?" Amos questioned "It's after 12, buddy", and he pointed at the clock on the wall. "Got to keep us fuelled with those calories, man." Davis then asked Phillip if he knew of any hotels that would be cheap and close by. "The Galmont would be your best bet. It's cheap. Down by the harbour, my Dad and his brother stay there when they go away on fishing trips. We'll check it out after lunch." So they all had lunch together and shared their steaks with my Dad and they told him a few of their army stories.

Davis said that the Americans had to come over and train them how to use some of the new flight equipment, he told Dad how one day they were talking about cars and one of the Yanks said he had a Cadillac back home that was giving him problems and the mechanic was looking around $120 to fix it. Davis explained that his Dad had a similar motor and, given that his father was a mechanic, offered to show him how to make basic repairs on it. He and Phillip took the American into one of the garages where there was an old chevy parked.

Davis clambered under the car. "Now the first thing you do, is take a spanner." "Spanner?" The Yankee replied. "What's a spanner, man?" "You know the tool you use to tighten or wrench out nuts and bolts?" "Oh, you mean a wrench! Haha. You Irish boys crack me up." Davis said he moved himself out from under the car and he and Phillip just stared at each other, as if to say. "If WWIII breaks out, these are the bastards that are going to have to save us." So after they finished their steaks they all went to the Galmont and surely enough Tiernan was standing outside having a smoke. Charlie thanked all three of them and went on his way.

Tiernan clocked him getting out of the truck. "Thank fuck, Charlie! We didn't know where you'd got to last night. I'll go get Friel" Tiernan went into the hotel and came out moments later with with Charlie Friel. "Jesus, Charlie! You gave us quite a scare. We searched everywhere for you." "Well you didn't search too fucking hard" my Dad replied "Cause I was in the closet." "Now, Charlie" Friel grinned "You're a big boy, you can take care of yourself." "What happened to no good man gets left behind?" My Dad snapped back.

"Do you consider yourself a good man, Charlie boy?"

"Fuck off, Friel."

Chapter 15

Save Stinker

When my Dad was expelled from school following the bust-up between his uncles and the principal, his mate Stinker stayed on to do his O-Levels but performed abysmally. He was big and strong, and well… that was about it. He did a lot of odd jobs for locals that his family knew such as painting, tiling and mainly farmwork that made the most use of his raw strength, anything to keep him out of the pub on weekdays. However one thing about Stinker, is that he had the gift of the gab. My Dad said to me that he could sell shite to his Grandma and convince her that it was sugar. One day he managed to acquire a pretty lucrative job selling TVs for Mr O'Leary; a respected salesman within the community.

Now selling TVs in Strabane was by no means an easy task. Even though by the 1960s, 75% of British homes had a television (you could probably half that when it came to rural communities in places such as Ireland), the people of Strabane were very much rooted in their ways. They were traditional folk that embraced the outdoors. Why would they want to spend all their free time huddled around a flashing box when they could be out mingling and enjoying the craic with the townsfolk? However, one thing that appealed to the men back then, and arguably appeals to most men nowowadays are two things: Women and football.

Strabane was as passionate about the GAA as any other district in Ireland but they had a fondness for the football over in England. Manchester United and Northern Ireland legend George Best was a particular appeal. My Dad had saw him play live once when he was with the Playboys in Scotland in an international game. Northern Ireland won 1-0 and my Dad said he carried the team on his back. The things he said he could do with a football back then were nothing short of astonishing. Imagine then the thrill both older and younger generations would get to experience seeing him complete his mazy dribbles and banging volleys played out right out in front of them from the comfort of their homes? Now we come to the women, in rural communities in Ireland there were without doubt natural beauties, but some of the talent on show over in England and America was incredible, particularly with actresses such as Elizabeth Taylor and Marilyn Monroe that were on the big screen.

My Dad said that he, Stinker and 2 other lads went to see "The Seven Year Itch" featuring that famous scene where Marilyn Monroe gets her white dress blown upwards standing over a subway grate by a passing train. He told me when they saw that scene their jaws damn near hit the floor. So the market was there and although it would be tricky, Stinker was the man. He took to his new job like a duck to water. He would brag about his accomplishments in the pub, claiming how one week he had managed to shift 6 TVs, including one to Mr. Olwell who hadn't even saw what a camera looked like, let alone a television. But as was always the case with Stinker, there was a catch. You see, Stinker was a wheeler dealer, in the sense that he would do anything to pocket some extra dough.

My Dad even told me how Stinker explained to him about 8 years ago that he felt a pain in his chest. He went to the doctors and they said to him "Liam, you've had a mini stroke. Most likely due to your reckless lifestyle of bingeing and drinking. You were lucky not to have a heart attack. If you keep this up, it will only end badly for you." My Dad said that Stinker thanked the doctor and walked solemnly out the door. But the second he left the hospital he rubbed his hands together in glee. "Happy days!" He exclaimed "More DLA, a feed of pints are on the menu tonight!". Yep, that was Stinker. So as it turns out, Stinker was selling the TVs at an inflated price, pocketing the extra money and then returning to his boss claiming he had sold them off for the original price.

He got away with it for about a month until Mr O'Leary was stopped on the street by one of the locals. "Bought one of your TVs there last week. £99 is pretty pricy for a picture box but it's some job all the same." The asking price for that model was £70. Mrs Williamson then confronted Mr O'Leary in his store, complaining that the colour TV she had bought, which of course was considerably pricier than black and white for £149 kept cutting out. The price of colour TVs was £100. Now Mr O'Leary was a very serious, and as I mentioned, a well- respected man who didn't like having his name or reputation tarnished in any way, so not only was Stinker fired, Mr O'Leary wanted to make an example out of him- by getting the police involved.

So after Stinker was fired he was drowning his sorrows down the local with my Dad and his mates when two officers walked in the door. Stinker knew instinctively that they were there for him so he got up and legged it to the bathroom. He sat in the toilet cubicle, with his feet tucked up on the toilet seat, like a truant school girl trying to avoid a teacher. The officers approached my Dad and his two pals. "We're looking for a Liam McAuley. Someone told us we could find him down here. Any of you folk seen him?" "Nope" was my Dad's response ."Haven't seen him" replied Daniel. "Who, Stinker?" chirped in Sean. "Yeah, he's just nipped off to the bathroom." The officers brushed past the lads and made their way towards the men's.

My Dad clashed Sean on the back of the head. "Fucking idiot." They entered the toilets and one of them banged on the cubicle door. "Liam William McAuley! Open up! You're under arrest for fraud!" Stinker sighed. "I'm coming, I'm coming." So Stinker was thrown in jail, and couldn't even come close to affording the bail money. So what was he to do? Well fortunately, he had my Dad and his buddies to help. They started a makeshift campaign. "Save Stinker" where they implored the locals, out of the good of their hearts to donate what they could, claiming he was wrongfully imprisoned for a 'misunderstanding' involving the asking prices of the TVs he was selling. Obviously, they took heed to avoid the parts of town where Mr O'Leary and his associates were known, but after a few weeks they managed to accumulate enough cash to bail Stinker out.

However Stinker wasn't going to let this lie. Now because of this whole incident, he and my Dad were flat broke but one day they were absolutely gagging for a pint, and Stinker spotted the two officers walking down the street one day. "I need to sort something out here, Mac" he said and went strutting up towards the two officers. "Stinker, would you get back here?! You'll be thrown in the clink again!", my Dad bellowed before ducking into a nearby brush. There was no way he was sharing a cell with Stinker's fat ass.

Stinker approached the officers. "Right, muckers. Me and my pal haven't eaten in two days, and I know for a fact youse have pocketed some of that bail money. So give us a tenner so we can go and get something to eat."

The two officers glanced at each other. "Liam…" one of them said. "I could easily throw you back into the brig, but I could not be bothered with having to drag you in and go through all that paper work." He took out his wallet and handed him a tenner. "Now get out of my sight!" 'By Christ…' my Dad thought as he watched on. 'How'd he manage that?!' I told you he had the gift of the gab, although on this occasion he was more direct and abrupt than eloquent. Times were still difficult though for Stinker, he was hardly qualified to do any meaningful work to begin with, and now that word got round that he was a rather unscrupulous character he found a solid job virtually impossible to come by. The locals ribbed him constantly as well. Whenever he passed someone that recognised him on the street they would shout " Save Stinker!" and one day a man came into the pub with a white shirt that had 'Save Stinker!" written on it in black marker and a hand-drawn image of Stinker's face. So Stinker decided that there was no longer a place for him in Strabane and decided to move away across the water, though this would be far from the last we'd see of him.

Chapter 16

Stinker in London

After travelling to England following the television scam fiasco, Stinker got a low-paid job loading crates onto boats and lorries for his uncle Bobby who owned a bar over in London, its name my Dad could not recall but it was fairly popular with the locals and former England striker Les Ferdinand was apparently a frequent flyer during his time with QPR. Bobby noticed how Stinker was able to load crates twice as heavy and at a much faster rate than the rest of the men. He also had more stamina, he drunk like mad but wasn't as addicted to cigarettes, which could not be said for the rest of the workforce as they were pausing every 5 minutes for a smoke break. Dad then told me that his uncle basically just said to him that he was willing to offer him a 10% wage increase to drive to the suppliers, and load and distribute crates of beer. How could he say no? So Stinker accepted the offer and that it was he worked as for a year and a half. Now his uncle was an old man, and getting frailer by the day. He used to be in and around the pub 6 days a week, but as his health declined he visited less and less often and was soon too weak to even leave his house. He was a widower and had no children, and it was Stinker who would have to make him his breakfast in the morning and his evening tea. Before he passed, one of his final actions was to sign the pub over to Stinker, who had always been good at giving orders as well as receiving them (unless of course somebody else came along with a better offer) and so agreed he would run the pub in Bobby's absence.

It had been 3 years since my Dad and Stinker had laid eyes on each other since he unceremoniously left. The Playboys had finished their tour of the pubs in various regions of the Gaeltacht and were now in England for the first time. It was like taking a step through a portal going from Ireland in the 80s to England at that time.

Tribes of new trendy, hip groups that evolved from popular music culture as Goths, High Camp and New Romantics were on the scene. Influencers like Boy George and David Bowie saw people sporting what now would be considered the fashion faux pas of shoulder pads, poodle hair, elaborate hats and giant hula hoop earrings. The lads decided to have a quiet night out, and walking down the street, Benjamin spotted a guy with a black top hat and white shirt, beige blazer and purple bow-tie, with him were two other fellas.

One had his head shaved save the gigantic spikes protruding from the front to the back of his head and the other guy was wearing a denim jacket with the sleeves ripped and two different kinds of earrings that dangled from his lobs, one of a crescent moon and one of a star. Benjamin leaned over and said to my Dad. "Now I don't know what the hell was in that last batch of weed we just smoked, but it looks like we've just walked into some fucked up flick of Willy Wonka's chocolate factory!".

They decided to head to a club. Again, the boys were in for a shock. A feverish night out in Ireland would consist of a load of beer, and a folk band playing all night with the pub floors bouncing and maybe a lock in. I had epilepsy as a child but it's a damn good thing my Dad didn't have it is what he said to me. They entered one of the clubs and found an empty booth. It was diagonal to the dancefloor and it was rammed with party-goers, it was almost as if they were all trying to clamber over the top of one another it was so congested. The strobe lights were bouncing off the walls, and the band on stage seemed to be doing more screaming than actual singing. They stayed less than an hour. This just wasn't their scene. The lads got a fish supper and then headed back to the hotel for the night.

The next morning they were to meet the owner of the bar that they were to be playing in that night. As the band bailed from the van, Stinker came out to greet them. When Dad and Stinker saw each other they were surprised to say the least. Both men had changed quite considerably in appearance over the 3 years. Stinker, who had little hair to begin with was now completely bald and my Dad had put on a serious amount of weight. He said it was cause the lads drunk like crazy, had terrible diets (he told me that they would often snack on Tayto's cheese 'n' onion crisps, particularly when the munchies kicked in) and got no exercise, apart from lifting the heavy gear to and from the van. "Well what's this?" my Dad asked in astonishment "Liam McAuley! What the fuck have you been doing with yourself?!" Stinker explained the whole situation and how he was too ashamed to be seen in and around Strabane. "Jesus, Stinker! You could have at least said goodbye." "I'm not very good at goodbyes, Mac, but I'm decent with hellos", and he held out his hand for my Dad to shake.

Dad introduced Stinker to Friel and the band and Stinker welcomed them inside. He said the bar was larger than any venue they had ever played in, there were two separate bar areas, a front and back and two stages, the main stage and a smaller one near the corner. Stinker introduced the men to the staff: the two bar ladies. A pretty blonde girl from America and a short-haired brunette beauty who hailed from Liverpool, and the two bar-men; Chris and Derek; who were in a relationship with one another.

The 1980s was a period of intensified homophobia which was sanctioned from the top echelons of society: the government, church, police and tabloids. The Conservative government of Margaret Thatcher was at war with the LGBT community and launched a series of homophobic and sexist moral crusades under the themes of 'family values' and 'Victorian values'. Obviously it would be safer with the ever-growing cultural night-life revolution for homosexuals to say walk down the street hand in hand and to attend parties and functions together but still, it was a precarious time and no-body outside the bar knew of their relationship.

The good thing about Stinker was that he couldn't give a toss about cultural, ethical or lifestyle differences, with the exception of loyalists and the monarchy, by God did he hate the monarchy. When me, my Mum, sisters and aunts went on a trip to London we visited Madame Tussauds and my Mum got a picture standing next to the waxworks of the Queen and King Charles. The photo still sits in my old home in Bellaghy Park. She is standing in a very upright manner with one hand behind her back, almost as to impersonate being a member of the royals herself. When Stinker visited us once he saw the framed photo and went in front of me and my Dad. "It's a shame, that of all the photos of that trip to London you had to get framed, you chose the one with your wife standing beside THAT black bastard!", and pointed to the Queen. So they spent the day together and then night fell.

There was a good crowd in, a lot of older ones mainly because as mentioned beforehand, the more exuberant youths of the day were heading to the clubs rather than pubs for a traditional Irish night of music. There were still quite a few young folk in, some you could tell were originally from Ireland by the way they talked and others were simply intrigued to hear some traditional music from across the water. The night went well, with some of the Irish boys taking the hands of timid English girls and showing them how to do an Irish jig. Once the gig was over my Dad went to the bathroom and came back to leave his bass back in the changing area when he saw the two bar-girls standing. In-front of them was a small coffee table and three lines of cocaine.

The girl from Liverpool spoke up. "There you go, Charlie. That's for me", she inhaled the line, "that one's for Becky" and Becky in turn did her part. "And that one's for you." My Dad said he froze. Yeah, he obviously dabbled with weed but cocaine? No. He didn't like what he saw it do to people. It didn't seem to be doing much harm to the girls. Stinker then came walking in. "What the fuck do youse think youse are doing?! If any of that shite's spotted around this bar we'll be shut down! Now get your arses back out there! There's plenty of punters waiting." He turned to my Dad. "Sorry about that, Charlie" He then knelt down and inhaled the line himself and brushed his nostrils. "But you know how this business goes." He patted my Dad on the back and left the room, with my Dad still standing in shock.

The next day Charlie decided that he wanted to say a proper goodbye to Stinker before the band moved on, so the van stopped off at the bar. Much to Dad's confusion, there were two suitcases at the front of the entrance and shortly after they pulled up, Stinker came walking out. My Dad and Friel hopped out. "What's going on, Stinker?" my Dad asked "I'm leaving", he swiftly replied. "And I want to come with youse. I'll be your roadie. I can lift gear twice my size, and I'll do it in double-quick time, saving you lot having to break your backs every-time you want to get set-up. I spoke to Chris, who's worked with me and my uncle for over 4 years and he's going to take the owl girl off my hands. I'm sick of this life, Mac. I want to see more of the country".

Friel took a few seconds to ponder. "I don't know." He contemplated. "We run a tight ship here. I can't be affording any trouble. Charlie, can you vouch for this man?" The incident involving the TV sales flashed through my Dad's mind and he took a quick glance at Stinker. "For sure, there'll be no problem." "Good" said Friel. "Well Liam, welcome aboard. Now gather your things and hop on in there through the back of the van."

Chapter 17

God Save the Queen

The Playboys had made their way throughout the local villages and towns of the southern provinces of Ireland and had now mad their way to Scotland. They pitched up in Glasgow and were playing at a few local bars when a representative from the Rangers Supporters club came calling. They were looking for a frontman to play a few numbers for the annual get together. Friel shut him down immediately. No way would a bunch of Nationalist Catholics be caught dead in a place like that. He told him he'd be hanging about till late afternoon if he decided to change his mind. Friel more or less slammed the door in his face.

My Dad was siting strumming a few chords in the hotel room when he caught wind of the conversation and chirped up after the man left. "Here, Charlie, why'd you turn him down. It'll be good money and you know them sort of fanatics will pack the place out." "It's the principle of the matter, Mac", Friel quipped. "Associating with them rabble of bastards would only bring our name into the firing line.

No one in nationalist areas will ever want us to set foot in their bars if they hear we did a show for Rangers supporters." My Dad mulled over things for a minute and then had a light bulb moment. "How about this here? I'll go there solo and do a few numbers for them, play to the crowd, get paid and I'll keep half of the dough, and the other half I'll hand over to the Playboys. The band name doesn't have to be brought into the matter."

Friel scratched his head "I suppose… if you feel you'd be up for it. But Charlie you'd have to be so careful. Everything you say, your religion, political views. It could get nasty if they catch wind of where you're from."

"Don't worry about it" my Dad replied. "If anybody asks. I'll lie about where I'm from. Simple as that." So Friel got in touch with the representative and the night was booked.

The following night my Dad and a young local boy called Alan, who would act as his roadie for the night cause as I mentioned Stinker despised the monarchy and wouldn't piss on anyone to do with the Rangers establishment if they were on fire, made their way into the supporters club. They came in round the back and a tall fellow in a navy blazer was there to greet them He shook their hands and led them into the backstage area, where there were 3 club officials were waiting for them.

One of them recognised Alan. "Ah, Alan, did yer da ever get a buyer yet for that moto'bike of his?" "Naw, not yet" the scruffy lad replied. "I kept telling 'im he's ginnae have to lower the price if he wants someone to take it aff his hands. Particularly with the amount of miles she has on her." One of the lads then eyed up my Dad. "You're the musician then? What's your name, son?" "Charlie" my Dad replied. "Where ye' from?" My Dad panicked. Should have probably have thought up a backstory but thinking things through at this age wasn't his style. "Belfast" he blurted out. "Strange", the third chipped in "I know two lads from Belfast and you sound nothing like them."

Dad paused for a moment. "Well, my Dad was from Strabane in the north and it was my mum who was from there. We moved when I was quite young. "Well that clears that up then" The fellow in the blazer said. He ran through the songs my Dad would be playing, he had handed Friel a copy of them the day before. Fairly basic traditional tunes and he was set to go on in half an hour. Until then, he was free to enjoy the open bar. He guzzled 4 pints in him in the space of about 20 minutes and mingled with the locals, talking about football and trying best to steer clear of politics but any Celtic or Ranger supporter will tell you, it's virtually impossible to do so when discussing the Old Firm. So he went up on stage and played to the crowd.

There wasn't much pressure on him to be honest as the numbers were high but a lot of them weren't listening intently. It wasn't like the other shows where the Playboys name was plastered at the front of the bar. This was just one man and his guitar, so he played, the crowd enjoyed it, and everything went without a hitch. He was sitting in the back area when one of the men in blazers came in. "Good performance, Charlie. They seemed to like your style." "That's if they even noticed me", my Dad chuckled.

My Dad didn't care about showmanship. As long as the people who employed him and the audience were satisfied, that was good enough for him. He had his guitar and the gear packed up and he and Alan were ready to head on their way when the man stopped them. "Oh Jesus, Charlie. I almost forgot. It's tradition at the end of the night to have a rendition of the British national anthem: 'God Save the Queen'. You know how to play it don't you?" 'Fuck' my Dad thought, 'now I'm rumbled'. He had to think on his feet again. "Oh I know it for sure, but I'm unfamiliar with the chords. You couldn't show me could you?" The man pulled up a tape recorder and played him the anthem. Fairly simple. 'God save our gracious queen...noble queen...send her victorious, happy and glorious...'. So my Dad agreed to do it, but to spit in the face of his culture, there would come a price. "Sure, I'll do it. If you throw in them 2 bottles of vodka there", he said, pointing to two clear bottles stocked up high on the adjacent shelf. "Not a problem. I'll fetch them now." So my Dad went out and spoke into the microphone. "I'm now going to round off the night with the national anthem of Britain. "God Save the Queen."

The crowd erupted into cheers, and everybody in the club now took notice. They set down their pints and stood up. Some with their arms around each other's back, others with their hands on their hearts and my Dad belted out the anthem with the whole building vibrating as the crowd sang along. He got the most thunderous applause of the night and people were whistling and cheering. To be fair though, if you had trained a goat to bleat it out they probably would have reacted the same way.

So my Dad made my way back to the hotel and all the lads were tucking into a KFC bucket. "Well, Charlie. How'd it go?" Friel asked. "Aye, not so bad. Had to sing God Save the Queen there at the end which made things tricky." Stinker nearly choked on his wing. "You did what?! Sang God Save the Queen to them shower of shites?!" "Ack sure you know, Stinker" Tiernan weighed in. "It's all part of the service ye know?" My Dad, Friel, Benjamin and Fergus all chuckled. "Come on", my Dad said beckoning towards the door. "I'll buy you a pint down at the hotel bar and fill you in on all the craic."

Chapter 18

Another Boomin' Christmas

It was a bitter cold winter's night in mid-December. Dad, Stinker and their buddy Darren were playing poker in Darren's small cottage just outside Strabane. They were huddled together around a small wooden table with the fire burning away in the hearth. Darren sat in his armchair whilst Dad and Stinker had two wooden chairs pulled in from the kitchen.

They had been playing for a couple of hours when Darren's wife Angela came in from the cold. "Jaysus! It would nip the fingers clean off your hands out there!" she bellowed as she shook off the snow. "Right Liam, Charlie?" "How's it going, Angela?" my Dad said as he raised his hand. "We've got ourselves a right shit-show going on for the town Christmas dance" she chirped "We're without a tree." "No tree at a Christmas dance? That is a right bollocks" Stinker weighed in. "The road from the local forest where we get all the trees is shut off due to the snow, so there's no way of getting it near 3 mile up the road to the parish hall."

Events such as these would usually have taken place in the Strabane Town Hall which was conveniently located about a 5 minute walk from the forest. The structure had been used as the offices and meeting place of Strabane Urban District Council, until it was destroyed by a bomb in 1972. "We'll get it someway, don't fret" her husband said. The four of them pondered for a while, then Stinker had another one of his legendary light bulb moments. "Hey, why don't we just carry the fucker?" The three of us could shift it up the road no bother." "That's a thought, Stinker" Darren replied. "Could we get it through all that snow is the thing?" "It'd not be a patch on youse!" Angela yelled. She had a habit of speaking in an elaborate, almost Shakespearean manner. "It's settled then" Stinker confirmed. "The three of us will cart it up the street and Cinderella shall go to the ball."

The following night was the evening of the gala. Dad, Darren and Stinker had positioned themselves with the tree outside the impound. They decided that since Stinker was the biggest that he should bear the brunt of the tree's weight on his back. Darren and Dad would clasp the tree from each side and they would walk at a steady pace.

It was tight going for the first few paces but eventually they established a rhythm, though trudging through thick snow was by no means an easy feat, and they had to watch out for patches of black ice that made the journey all the more hazardous. What also didn't help matters is that Stinker had decided on this particular evening not to wear a belt, and so would stop every 100 odd yards or so to readjust his jeans to stop them from falling down. "For the love of fuck, Stinker!" my Dad yelled from the side. "If we keep going at this rate we won't be there for next year's dance never mind tonight!" "For God sake's, Mac! There's twigs going up my arse!"

They continued their faltering progress and eventually the parish hall was in sight. A couple of kids were having a snowball fight and a few of them thought it would be a lark to ping a few balls in the direction of our three tree bearers. Dad and Darren were struck, whilst Stinker remained relatively unscathed (bar the twigs up his arse) as he was protected in the majority by the foliage of the tree. "Wee bastards!" Darren barked over the hail of balls. They made their way up the steps and brought the tree into the hall. Cheers greeted the three, some my Dad said seemed genuine, others were perhaps ironic given the fact that the dance had already started and some were perhaps ironic given sight of these three jesters stumbling in with a tree covered in snow.

Darren's wife Angela, dressed in her finest approached them. "Well done, darlings!" she said shrilly and gave them each a kiss on the cheek. The event organiser came up to inspect the tree. Needless to say, it wasn't in a great shape. Many of its branches were frayed, and a lot of the foliage had been lost with my Dad and Darren gripping onto it so tightly. Plus the greenery that had been pressed up against Stinker's back was now out of sync with the rest of the tree. "That'll be £70", Stinker said to the man.

Angela had agreed payment for the lads' services before they set out. Dad and Darren would each get a twenty and Stinker would pocket thirty given the fact that it was his idea to carry the tree in the first place. "You must be joking" the thin man with a crooked nose scoffed "That's not a tree, that's an overgrown house plant. Look at the state of it!" "Listen, buddy" my Dad intervened "We've just carried that damn thing near 3 mile through the snow and now you're gonna say it's not acceptable?!" "We could stick it in the corner I suppose, but there's no way I'm paying for it." He snapped back. "Then the tree's coming with us!" Stinker barked back. "Come on, fellas."

The three reassumed their tree carrying positions but the organiser beckoned the security at the door over and the men were ushered out, along with Angela who kicked up a fuss over how downright disrespectful and indecent Mr. Johnston was being. The four of them were stood out in the freezing cold. "Well that was one waste of a fucking night!" Darren declared. Meanwhile, Angela was still arguing with the security at the door. "Get that weedy bastard out here now till I give him a piece of my mind!" she shrieked. "Leave it love, will ya?" Darren said as he escorted her away from the door.

The four began ambling back to Darren's through the snow when Stinker stopped by at a phone box "The bastards aren't getting away with it. Not a chance." Stinker was never one to let a grudge lie, as was evidenced with his encounter with the two police officers that arrested him a few years ago. "Who you calling, Stinker?" my Dad enquired. Stinker gave no response. But he did hear the subject of the call Stinker was making. "Hello, Police? Yeah, I've just left the Christmas dance taking place at Strabane parish hall and noticed two lads leaving what appeared to be a suspect device wrapped in a cloth underneath one of the tables by the main stage! Please hurry!" He then slammed the phone down. "You're a mad bastard!" Darren said with a look of bewilderment but at the same time respect at Stinker's sheer audacity.

Dad just kicked some snow and shook his head. He knew since his school days what Stinker was capable of. Angela was getting herself in a tizz. "Liam! You didn't! The authorities aren't going to find anything! We'll be done for wasting police time!" "And just how will they know it was us?" Stinker chuckled. He turned and began walking back towards the hall. "Where are you going, sir?" my Dad called out. "To get my present!" Stinker shouted back. "It is nearly Christmas after all!" "I better go after the eejit" my Dad said to Darren. "You two head on home." He shook Darren's hand and Angela gave him a hug. "Take care, Charlie, and Merry Christmas."

Stinker and Dad stopped just across the hall and waited for a few minutes. Surely enough an army truck came speeding down the road and stopped just outside the hall. Six soldiers jumped out and stormed the building. From the inside shrieks of horror could be heard as orders were shouted for everyone to clear out. Party goers, all dressed in their best were funnelled out onto the streets as they looked at one another in confusion at just what the hell was going on. Surely enough Mr. Johnston was led out by the arm by a soldier in a red beret.

He was utterly incandescent at the thought of his well-planned night now reduced to tatters. "For the love of God! There's no bomb in the hall! Why can't you see everyone at this dance has paid for tickets and I know personally?!" He then clocked my Dad and Stinker across the road. "Them! It was them two! They've got it in for me cause I wouldn't pay them for their bloody tree! "You two!" the soldier shouted. "Over here, now!" My Dad and Stinker sauntered over. The soldier had a stern and uncompromising face and he glared at the pair as if he was trying to burn a hole through them with his eyes. "One of you make a call about a suspect device being dropped off at this establishment?" "No!" my Dad said with authority, cause at least for his part it was true. "Not a chance" Stinker called out. "I know this man, though.

He's harboured some bitterness towards me after I advised him to spend a pretty penny on a horse that fell flat down at Aintree. Plus our two owl' boys never saw eye to eye." Stinker wasn't particularly bright, but he had street smarts, and could think on his feet. "That's a fucking lie!" Mr. Johnston blurted out "I never even met this man before tonight. He's talking absolute rubbish!" The soldier didn't know who to believe, but at the end of the day, he didn't have time to play truth or lies, and this was an incident that the army wouldn't exactly want recorded in the books. Plus, this was the 80s.

There was no way to track who made the call that night from a phone box. "The three of you, out of my sight! Now!". He summoned his men and they clambered back into the truck. "You utter bastard!" Mr Johnston seethed. "Ruin MY night because I wouldn't pay you for a fucking tree!" He stared Stinker up and down but wouldn't dare get physical. Stinker was twice his size and had my Dad for back up. "Make sure you get home safe now" Stinker said as he turned and walked away.

As my Dad walked alongside him, he was still trying to comprehend the situation. "Do you think you might have gone a bit far, Stinker? I mean, all that rabble cause he wouldn't fork out for a piece of shit tree." "The man and his friends treated us with nothing but disrespect the second we walked into that joint, Charlie." Stinker said calmly "Not even a word of thanks for carrying the fucking thing 3 miles in the blistering snow. People like that need to learn, you can't go around treating others with disrespect all the time and expect to walk away unscathed." There's truth in those words. A lesson needed to be learned, and by God did Mr Johnston learn it the hard way.

Chapter 19

The shoe-shit incident

The Playboys had just finished another gig, this time in Derry, and were back having afters with a few of the other bands. Friel was chatting to the dignitaries of the night. I say dignitaries, it wasn't exactly a shirt and tie scenario but many of them were from bars in and around Ulster, so it was good to get the Playboys name out there. My Dad, Tiernan, Benjamin, Fergus and of course Stinker were at the bar guzzling pints and discussing how they think the gig went "I was sweating like a horse!" my Dad announced to the lads.

My Dad for all the years I knew him would sweat quite profusely when performing. That's why he always had a towel nearby. I recall one time in the Dunloy parish hall when he was in his later years and performing with the Comhaltas he asked me to go fetch a towel from the car because after only a couple of songs he was sweating quite a bit.

I remember some of the younger girls playing the fiddle laughing at the sight, which I didn't find very tasteful. "It's this packed in bar" Fergus the drummer claimed, "sure just look at my armpits!" he held his arms aloft to reveal two massive circular sweat patches saturating his shirt. "For fuck's sake, Fergus put your arms down! There's women watching." "You lot think youse had it bad?!" burst out Stinker. "I had to lug them bastardin' speakers all the way up them rickety steps." "Sure that's the job you're getting paid to do" smirked the keyboard player Benjamin as he rolled a cigarette.

It was Benjamin who showed my Dad how to make a cigarette from scratching using papers and tobacco. I'd seen him do it about the house, although sometimes it wasn't tobacco he used. It was the green stuff. 'Herbal remedies' I believe is what he told me it was when I asked why it wasn't brown like the other stuff when I was 8 or 9. It seems to take quite a bit of time and dexterity to roll a neat one. I see the old hands about the Village Inn do it sometimes. It involves spreading the tobacco in just the right amounts across the paper, rolling it up gently and then licking the edges to seal it and eventually wrap it into place.

At least that's how I think it goes. Never was into smoking myself, never saw the appeal of it. It rots your teeth, leaves your breath stinking, gives you ugly stains on the tips of your finger and above it all, it doesn't even have a pleasant taste. Even though the new craze of vaping is just as bad for you because of all the chemicals and the fact that it gives you 'popcorn lung', at least it leaves a refreshing strawberry and watermelon after scent. The only time I've smoked is to impress pretty girls outside of nightclubs. "Yeah, be that as it may" Stinker retorted. "I still don't get paid enough.

Speaking of which, I'm flat out of doe. Whose round is it?" The other four soon discovered that between them all they barely had enough left to scrape together for a pint. "Fuck sake. Clean out all five of us" Tiernan said. "S'pose we could just ask for free drink from the bar?" The ever crafty Stinker suggested "We did play for them nearly all night". "WE?" piped up Tiernan "You mean 'us'. We're the ones who played whilst you sat scratching your fat hole!" "Settle you down T-boy, I think there's a hair out of place" Stinker snapped back and with that the always vain Tiernan wiped back his black mop, just to be sure. "Alright boys, take it easy" Fergus interjected. "Don't sweat it chaps" Benjamin quipped from behind his cigarette. "I mean, anymore than youse have already done tonight, and besides, Friel towl us we're not to be scoping for free drink.

Trying to establish a decent reputation for the band around these bars and we can't do that if we suck the place dry." "So what do we do then?" my Dad asked "Go ask Friel." Benjamin suggested "He's never short of a pound or two." "Why me?" Dad didn't like to come off as a scrounger. He'd been grinding ever since his uncles got him booted out of school and wasn't the sort for asking for handouts. "Cause you're the newest member of the band, that's why." "Well what about, Stinker?" my Dad enquired "You're joking, right?" Tiernan butted in "I think he meant newest member who's actually worth a fuck" "Right!" Stinker jumped up. "I'm not putting up with that shite from a cocky little prick like you. I'll snap ye in half!" Tiernan and Stinker never really saw eye to eye.

He was young and bold. Stinker was older, but just as bold. Tiernan cared about appearances and thought Stinker should too. He had confided in my Dad that he had asked Friel could they not have just hired some other big lug to do his job instead, someone cleaner and a bit more respectable. Dad never told Stinker this. How could he? Stinker would have bust Tiernan up in about two seconds. "Settle down, Stinker" my Dad said as he tried to defuse the situation. "I'll go ask Friel if he'll lend us enough for another round."

Dad left the table and approached Friel as he was just finishing talking to an older fellow in a brown blazer. "Charlie." He said as Friel whirled around. "Yes Mac, what can I do for you?" "Me and the lads are absolutely gagging after that show there." "Yes" Friel stated "It is a bit cramped in here, and it's a summer's evening after all." "Well, we were just wondering if you could spare a little something so we could get a quick pint in?" Dad quickly glanced at the top pocket of Friel's jacket.

That's where he kept all the band money and had seen him on numerous occasions, including tonight, whipping notes out and buying drinks for other folk in the bar. "Sorry, Charlie boy. No can do. I've coughed up enough dosh, licking the holes of the other bar owners tonight. You get your wages and you choose how to spend them, you use them up, it's not my problem."

Friel was for the most part my Dad said, a sound fellow, but I suppose to be a manager in any department, you got to pick and choose how generous and in turn, how shrewd you are with money. "Come on, Charlie" my dad said back to Friel. "Could you not shell out something spare so we can get a fucking drink?" "Nope. Sorry, Charlie. Final answer."

My Dad just nodded and turned back towards the table with the rest of the band. "Well?" Stinker asked "He said no, the tight bastard" my Dad sulked. "Says we get paid what we get paid and if we spend it all that's our problem. Not his "Fuck me", Benjamin weighed in as he finished with his cigarette. "I know Friel's a stingy ball-licker but that takes the biscuit." "Did you tell him we were only after the one?" Tiernan asked. "Aye, I did. Still got nothing from him." "I suppose he has a point" big, friendly Fergus said to offer some perspective. "Maybe if we had spaced our drinks out, and made the money last then we wouldn't be in this hole." "Space our drinks out?!" Stinker shouted, who was absolutely livid. "In the name of fuck, we've been sitting here for the past two hours while arse-licking Friel goes around talking shite with all the higher ups and you think we should have spaced our fucking drinks out?!" "He has a point" Tiernan on this occasion reluctantly agreed with his adversary. "I mean.

What is there to do in a bar other than drink. I mean, I don't see many girls around here do you?" My Dad said he took a quick scope and what Tiernan said was true. It was all older folk at this particular bar. Some owl gents 60th so all the women there either pensioners or married. Not really ideal for any members looking to capitalise on any potential groupies who might be floating about. "Fuck it lads" my Dad said. "We'll call it a night." The five of them gathered their things and left. Dad gave Friel a quick tap on the shoulder to let him know they were heading back to the hotel. Friel told them he wouldn't be far behind.

The next morning my Dad said he and Tiernan were awoken in their room by a howl from out in the hall. "What dirty conniving, bastard would do something like that?!" Dad got out of his bed, pulled on his jeans and went to the door. Friel was standing outside of his room with his hand over his mouth, staring down at a single brown shoe that had been placed outside of his room. Inside the shoe, was a shit. Yes that's right.

A piece of human shit was sitting in the hole of the shoe. Friel knocked on Benjamin and Stinker's door. "Get out here now and look at this!" Soon all six of them had congregated out in the hall. All staring down at this shoe with a piece of shit in it. "Who in under fuck did that?" my Dad asked. "That's just pure rotten" Fergus winced. So the underlying question, that still remains unanswered to this day. Is who done it? Every member of the band denied playing any part in it. Surely it couldn't have been Fergus. Cause he was sharing the room with Friel. It wouldn't have been Tiernan cause like I said, he was all about appearances and the idea of this pretty boy taking a dump in a shoe doesn't really add up.

I lived with my Dad for the best part of 25 years and although he was capable of some pretty ballsy and outrageous acts, I don't think he would have went that far, although Friel had fucked him off with the way he spoke to him. That leaves Benjamin and Stinker. Not to sound biased but my money's on Stinker. The clue's in the nickname. Though if you wanted to be really diligent about the whole process I would have suggested asking all the lads to break out their shoes and deduct who's missing one or who has a shoe that resembles the one with the faeces in it. I would have made a good detective wouldn't have I?

Chapter 20

The 'panting dogs' and the dead dog

Another gig was in the bag, this time they had travelled to the largest town on the Isle of Skye in Scotland called Portree. The band were all sitting around a small table just outside the bar when three ladies approached them. One of them was considerably older than the other two. She wore a pastel coloured tank top and mini-skirt. The kind of thing I would see the girls wearing at the teen elk (a nightclub we went to when we were like 13) although Dad said she must have been at least 40. She had brown hair that was tied back in a long ponytail.

The girl to her left had curly ginger hair and was in a purple jumper. She wore maroon coloured boots and had a tattoo of a music note on her neck. She was wearing considerably less make-up than the other two, especially the older woman, who was caked in it. The third girl was slim, had black hair and wore blue jeans and a white-vest top. It didn't look very high end but she could pull it off because she was a real beauty, and caught Tiernan's eye immediately.

The older woman extended her hand out to Friel. "Nice to meet youse. Great show tonight." She had a very thick and broad Scottish accent. "I'm Theresa, and these two wee lasses are my daughters. Tracey and Alana." The two girls behind her waved. Everyone waved back, apart from Tiernan who just nodded towards them. I guess waving wasn't playing it cool enough for his liking. "Evening, girls" Friel said. "Why don't you three pull up a seat and you can tell us all about this fine town." "Nae bother." She shouted in the door. "Oi, Richy! (the barman) Bring us out three stools so we can have a natter way the band here. And fetch my jacket while you're at it! I'm freezing my tits off out here!" She was as a rough and ready woman you'll ever meet as my Dad described her. The stools were fetched and the three sat down next to them.

Tiernan of course used all of his cunning so he could be sat next to Alana. "You're bound to be cold as well, wearing nothing but a wee vest" he said, pointing beside himself as the stools were placed down. "The wind isn't blowing as harshly from this direction, you sit here. You'll be warmer." "Sure", she smiled back. So the nine of them were huddled around this small table out back, nattering and telling tales about where they're from and how Dad and Stinker became affiliated with the Playboys.

2 hours or so had passed when a slightly inebriated Friel stood up from the table. "Well ladies, it's been a pleasure chatting to youse, but we best head on. The drink's gone to my head and I need to fill my stomach with something before heading to bed, we're up early tomorrow to set out and I don't want to be dying from a hangover." "Leaving so soon?" Tracey asked. "That's the rock 'n' roll way, baby" Tiernan replied and winked in Alana's direction. "You'll stay for one more!" Theresa answered sharply. "No, no" grinned Friel "I couldn't take another one." "Who knew a bunch of fellas from Ireland would be such lightweights" smirked Alana. "I'm no lightweight!" declared Tiernan, with his chest puffed out. "Then you"ll come back to ours for a few before heading away!" cried out an adamant Theresa.

She had made her case, the lads weren't departing without having a few more with them, and she struck my Dad as the kind of woman who didn't like being said no to. "I'm up for it." Tiernan said. "Me too" declared Stinker. He was positioned beside Tracey, and as the drink flowed, the two seemed to be scooting closer and closer to one another. "Not a chance!" Friel scoffed. "We're to be up at 6.30am tomorrow. To be away for 7." "Aye, I'm wrecked" Benjamin agreed "And it's hard enough getting Stinker out of his pit when he's sober." "Who's Stinker?" asked Tracey. "That fella there" pointed Benjamin. "Why do they call you that?" she chuckled. "It's just a nickname he's had since primary school, my Dad interjected, cause you see…" "Fuck up, Mac" snapped Stinker.

I mentioned in the first chapter that his nick-name was self-explanatory, his personal hygiene and the way he carried himself left a lot to be desired. My Dad said one day when they were staying in a room together he came out of the shower with a towel wrapped round him. My Dad winced and said. "Stinker, when I was a young boy working in the chicken factory clearing out hen shite I smelt some powerful things, but the stench coming off you takes the fucking biscuit!".

He grew to embrace the nickname. He had no choice, in rural communities, particularly in Ireland, once you get a nickname, it stuck. I could rhyme you off a list of lads whose nicknames I know before I could tell you their actual name: Minty, Clemy, Curry, Bones, Drogba. The list goes on. But on this particular occasion, Stinker did not want his nickname to become common knowledge. He had his eye set on Tracey and, well, would you want to get with a guy known as Stinker? " I'm beat, too" Fergus conceded. "And I could do with something to eat as well. Tell you what. Whoever wants to go wae' the girls can go and the rest of us can grab something and meet them back in the hotel once they're sorted."

Fergus always found a solution. "Aye sure that's grand" Friel said. "Right, folks, let's head out." Everybody stood up and Stinker tapped my Dad on the shoulder "You coming, Charlie?" "Yeah, sure." My Dad instantly responded. He would come to regret that decision. In fact, he regretted about a mile up the road when Tiernan had paired up with Alana, Stinker with Tracey and he was stuck with the loudmouth mother, who did not stop santering (talking) the whole journey back to their place. It was a pastel coloured flat that was located down just by the harbour. The six of them made their way inside.

In the living area there was a small two-seater sofa and in two corners of the room there were two single chairs. Tiernan had worked his charm on Alana and was sitting in one of them with her on his lap. Tracey was sitting in the other with Stinker kneeling beside her. Oh, joy! The sofa was Theresa and my Dad's then. They talked for a while but my Dad was growing increasingly uncomfortable with the situation. It was fine in the pub but here the atmosphere was slightly more intense. Her girls were occupied with men, and, judging by the way she was interacting with my Dad.

She wanted one too. She laughed heartily at nearly everything he said, even when he wasn't trying to be funny, and kept complimenting him on his long, wavy hair, running her hand through it. She paused the proceedings to grab a cigarette but discovered she was fresh out. "Oh, fuck!" she hollered "I'm bum out of ciggies!" "I'll run out and get you some!" my Dad immediately volunteered. "Aw, you're a wee pet" she said and kissed him on the cheek. He left the flat and went back down to the pub. He bummed a few cigarettes off a couple of young lads and made his way back to the flat. As he approached the door he could hear the faint sound of moans coming from inside.

He opened the door and made his way into the living area and what a sight he saw! The mother was standing in the middle of the living room with a cigarette in her mouth and in each corner Stinker and Tiernan were having sex with Tracey and Alana. Dad dropped the cigarettes. The mother seemed unbothered. What were they, a pack of fucking wolves?! "Ah, Charlie. I found these in my bedside drawer. You wouldn't fetch us a bucket of water for them panting dogs over there?" Dad didn't know where to look. "No bother, love." He spluttered. He turned and made his way back out of the flat and straight to the hotel. Getting felt up by a cougar and witnessing an orgy isn't what he signed up for when he joined the Playboys back in Strabane. Not by a bloody long shot.

The Playboys were back in Ireland. They had a week off from touring so my Dad and Stinker were visiting a friend of Stinker's in Magherafelt. Her name was Diane, and she lived in a small cottage with her husband Matthew, their two kids: Rachel and Stephen who were only primary school age, and their Jack Russell, that they called Baxter. Matthew was a lorry driver and was out making a delivery in the evening and everyone else was gathered in the living room. Diane was sat on a lounge chair whilst my Dad and Stinker took the sofa.

The kids were playing near the fireplace with the dog, who was rushing back and forth and yapping playfully as they tossed a hurling ball between one another. "So fellas." Diane said as she nursed a cup of tea on her lap. "How's life on the road with the band going?" "Aye, decent" Stinker replied "Lugging all that gear about isn't doing wonders for the owl' back. I shifted crates down at the docks when I was younger and I think it's catching up with me. Doctor says I should probably rest it more." "More?!" my Dad chortled "It takes you about an hour to get the gear out of the van and onto the stage and then you spend the rest of the time necking pints while we play!" Diane laughed.

"Well, you lazy fuckers could always do it!" Stinker snapped back. "Then you'd be out of a job you muppet" my Dad replied. "Oh, Charlie you're a wile one" she chuckled. "Charlie." Rachel called out "Yes, my dear" my Dad said back. "Why's your hair so long?" "You look like a girl." Stephen laughed. "That's cause he's a pansy" Stinker said as he pointed to him. "That, and he's too stingy to head to the barber's and get it chopped." "Coming from the baldy bastard who's not had a hair on his head since he was 21."

My Dad grinned as he rubbed Stinker's bald top. They all laughed. One thing me and my family all possess, is the ability to snap back so quickly when someone tries to get the one over on us. In my local pub the direction of exchange tends to go that 90% of the time it's just lads tearing each other to shreds. The rest of the time is spent talking about how shit work is, horses, the GAA or football. One afternoon I came in to watch the Celtic vs Aberdeen Scottish cup final. I stopped drinking in November 2024 and get ribbed for it constantly.

An Irish man who doesn't drink is like finding a bloody unicorn, particularly in rural villages. There's a comedy sketch show called. 'You know you're Irish when…' and one of the shorts is a guy walking up to a bar and the barman goes "What'll it be?" and he goes "7up please." The whole bar goes quiet and a woman just whispers to her friend. "Freak." But anyway, I came walking in and was not in the bar 10 seconds when one of the older fellows went. "Get a Diet Coke for that pussy there, he's parched." I immediately replied. "Better than being an alcoholic like you." I then said to his wife ."How long has he been in here for?" "Since about 12" she said. I looked up at the clock. "And it's just after 3. Good job" and winked at him.

One afternoon I was getting the bus home from school and a boy in year 8 tried to take the mic out of my sister who was in year 11. He fancied himself as a bit of a cool kid cause he hung around with a lot of year 12s. He stood up in the middle of the bus, put on a shrill voice and went. "Guess who I am? Christopher, oh, Christopher!" That was one of Rosie's friends. Now up until the age of about 15 this kid sounded like a gerbil when he spoke. My sister within 5 seconds replied "Guess who I am?" She then put on a squeaky voice. "Mousey, oh, Mousey!" (that was the nickname of one of the boys he hung out with in year 12) "Aye, get back to me when your fucking voice breaks."

The roar from the back of the bus was almost deafening. By the fireplace the kids continued to toss the ball back and forth. The dog kept leaping in the air, trying to catch it in its mouth. "So guys, what's the grand plan?" Diane asked "Youse are both past 30. You guys just going to travel with the band the rest of your lives? What about finding a nice woman? What about starting a family?" The two just looked at each other. "We hadn't really thought that far ahead" Stinker replied.

I've never been in a band so I don't fully grasp the mentality of musicians but I imagine a lot of the time, particularly when on tour, they just live from one gig to the next. Not so much nowadays with your modern pop singers like Beyonce or Katy Perry who get married and start families whilst they progress throughout their career. The lifestyle back in the 70s or 80s for bands was considerably more hedonistic. There's an interview back from years ago with Mick Jagger, and he's being interviewed by a very conservative English chap.

He asks him "How long do you give yourself just going from coast to coast being sort of… you know… just…" and Mick Jagger goes "I don't know… I never expected to be doing this for 2 years if I'm being honest with you…um…I think we're going to keep going for at least another year." Baxter the dog leapt in the air once again as the kids threw the ball and caught it this time. "No, Baxter, give that back!" Rachel shouted and reached her hand in and tore the ball out of the dog's mouth. The dog lunged forward and bit her on the arm. "Ow!" she squealed and burst into tears. "You wee bastard!" my Dad yelled and grabbed the dog by the scruff of the neck and launched it at the hearth.

The dog crashed head first and let out a yelp. It collapsed in a heap and my Dad said he spotted its tongue rolling out of the corner of its mouth. Oh fuck. "Charlie!" Diane shrieked "What have you done?!" "Baxter!" cried out Stephen. The mother ran across the room and rubbed its head. Yep. It was dead. Diane, Rachel and Stephen all started wailing. Back for A level Classical Civilisation I studied the Aeneid by Virgil which tells the story of Aeneas; the mythological founder of Rome.

In one chapter, his son: Ascanius is out hunting in the woods and he spots a deer. He is unaware that this particular deer is sacred to Silvia, who sees it more as her pet as it is a very tame creature and would merrily skip about children's feet and come up and eat berries straight out of the locals' hands. He kills it and she goes ballistic. She rounds up all the herdsmen and shepherds and they come after Ascanius. I can see similar parallels, as my Dad said Diane burst out the door and went screaming through the streets. "That bastard Charlie McNamee killed my dog!" My Dad and Stinker legged it out the back door. Where could they go to hide? Where else? The pub. They ducked into the local and each gave the barman a fiver to let them hide in the backroom. He agreed and they laid low for a while.

Eventually they heard a rabble of men entering the bar. "Hey, Daire." One of them called out. "You didn't happen to see two fellas come by here? A fat, bald cunt and a long haired bastard who goes by the name Charlie?" He paused for a second. My Dad and Stinker held their breath "No lads. I haven't. I just had a few chaps in earlier with their sons who had just finished their shifts, but they looked nothing like the fellas you described." The men mumbled to themselves and departed.

My Dad said he and Stinker hung around for another 10 minutes or so before leaving, just to be safe. Anyone from Northern Ireland will tell you that back in them days individuals from certain communities could be particularly volatile. The sort of folk who wouldn't think twice about bashing your head in and leaving you on the pavement. This was the Troubles after all…people had been killed for less.

Chapter 21

Physical Love

I'm going to have to stop giving my chapters such open-ended titles, cause I then feel compelled to explain what they are actually in reference to. Just like when I explained that the 'Discovered by the Playboys' chapter wasn't about the mansion full of lingerie models, I can tell you this chapter is not going to have anything in it like what those women in Scotland got up to but is the title of an original song my Dad recorded with the Playboys, along with a talented singer called Rhonda.

The Playboys were essentially a cover band, they weren't releasing a host of original tracks but one day a few of those responsible for promoting the band announced they had raised enough money to book a few sessions in a proper recording studio, and they wanted produce a track and get it out into the public scope over radio, thus furthering the image of the band. The Playboys wheeled up in their van outside a small building, almost like a cabin that had faded paint and a few cracks near the window, a makeshift sign labelled 'McFarlin's recording centre' was hung up over the door. Guess this was the place. Friel had been driving them around town for close to half an hour trying to find it.

The boys in the back of the van were frustrated cause Friel refused to stop and ask for directions, he kept saying, "Lads, I know Strabane like the back of my hand, it's nearby, no need to stop." Stinker also took up a considerable bit of room and Tiernan, who as I mentioned before, was never Stinker's biggest fan, didn't understand why, when all the equipment would be waiting for them at the studio, Stinker had to invite himself along.

A lady and a man were waiting for them in the car park once they pulled up, as they clambered out he came strutting across the park with a scowl on his face, but the girl, who walked just behind him seemed rather happy and cheerful. He was a short man, wearing a black blazer white shirt, navy trousers, and his hair was combed over to one side. He went straight up to Friel. "You're 15 minutes late, Charlie. We only have this spot booked for 3 hours and we need to get a shift on so hurry up!" He turned and paced towards the cabin and knocked on the door, a man answered and they began conversing.

The lady then stepped forward to introduce herself to the lads. She was a very tall woman, a good fraction over 6 foot and had long brown curly hair, she wore a denim jacket with a bright pink shirt underneath and sported a set of tall black zip-up boots, she shook every one of one of them by the hand. "Hi, my name's Rhonda. Sorry about Billy, he can be a tad impatient, likes things to be done on the button." From her accent you could tell she was a proper country girl, my Dad never found out but he told me she definitely had an American twang to the way she spoke. Like one of the girls you'd see touring the scene in Nashville.

My Dad guessed Billy was her manager. Billy then shouted over from the studio entrance. "Right, everything's set up, come on, get going!" None of the lads liked his attitude, he seemed like a pernickety little bugger. He had an elaborate silver watch on his wrist and every while or so my Dad said when they were recording he would dramatically thrust his arm out and gaze down at it. He always seemed to be wrapped up in his own sense of self-importance but the they all kept their heads down for the sake of the track. The studio on the inside, as reflected on the outside, was very modest.

There was one table placed on the centre of the room with two plain chairs beside it, diagonal to the booth was another table, this one had a pot of tea and a set of paper cups wrapped in kitchen foil. The booth itself took up the majority of the room, as here was where all the instruments, microphones and recording equipment was placed. The studio director Damien sat on a green, padded swivel chair and had a set of large headphones perched around his neck.

He beckoned the whole crew over. "Right folks, this is how it's going to work, we need to break the whole thing down into sequences, the instrumental comes in first and then who's singing the opening verse?" "That'll be this man" Friel said and patted my Dad on the back. "Good stuff" Damien replied, "now recording in a studio isn't like playing live, it can be quite a drawn out process, voices need to be synthesised and collaborated, and you have to be in constant harmony with the band's instrument players, otherwise the track will sound disjointed and foggy."

Stinker, during this chat had decided to help himself to a cup and lifted about 8 biscuits from the tray, no since in him listening in. "So when's the lovely lady coming into the track?" Damien asked and smiled at Rhonda. "We've arranged for her to be brought in after the repeat of "Physical Love". Billy the manager quipped in. "All right, lady and gentlemen, let's get cracking!" My Dad said to me you'd think recording a song would be a lot of fun. It wasn't.

Constantly being told to re-record certain verses, the pitch not being quite right, the keyboard instrumental sounding a bit off key, and of course that arsehole Billy weighing in with his two cents, he just hovered over Damien the whole time and kept quizzing him on what certain buttons do, and how they could improve the track's quality and give it more 'va-va voom.' My Dad said he got through about 12 cups of tea and 2 and a half packs of cigarettes in them 3 hours. He said the tiny studio was just a ball of smoke at one stage, if anybody had driven by and peered in the window, the fire brigade would have been rung.

After what felt like an eternity, the track was complete. I remember my dad letting us hear it on a CD he kept on one of the old CD players you used to get but it's long gone now. However, if you go onto YouTube you can hear a snippet of it. Type in 'The Playboys Through the years' and select the video with the yellow bunny in the red bow-tie. If you forward the video to approximately '1.43' you'll hear a jazzy piano intro and then my Dad belting out "#I wanna love you through the night!...# You can hear a part of Rhonda's segment too, she sings something like "#You walked all over me…Who do you think you are?#" So there track was going to be heard throughout the region, or so they thought.

This was during the Thatcher years, and conservatism was trumping any notions of radical expression or promoting bohemian lifestyles. The lyrics were provocative, too provocative to be played on radio. I guess they shouldn't have expected anything else, given the name of the title. I remember hearing a report on BBC Radio 1 about genres of songs and particular artists that were prohibited during the 80's and I guess 'Physical Love' falls into that category.

Therefore, I do not know why for the life of me my Dad thought it would be a good idea to let his Mum hear the track. She was a humble, closed off farming woman who had very rigid traditions and values. My Dad came lumbering into her room one afternoon with a big cassette player and a cassette of the track. As he was placing it in, his Mum seemed thrilled. "My Charlie! A big-time singer!" My Dad hit play and the cassette began to whir into life. His Mum was probably expecting to hear an eloquent, sentimental song about the flowers blooming in spring or the scenic sights of the Glens of Antrim. My Dad's verse kicked in "#I wanna love you through the night…Don't wanna see you through the day#… "Wait hold on a second" my Granny said and my Dad stopped the track. "What was it you just said?" My Dad swallowed.

He knew he had made a mistake "Um… Don't wanna see you through the day" My Granny gritted her teeth. "So it goes, I want to love you through the night but don't want to see you during the day?" There was a tense five second pause "Yeah, pretty much". My Granny's eyes widened "HALLION!" she cried and launched a cushion at my Dad's head. She then got off her armchair and went for the tall broom leaning in the corner. Time to bail. My Dad bounced off the sofa and bolted out the back door, my granny made a feeble attempt to chase him for a while but soon gave up as he tore up the path. I guess a genius is never appreciated in his own time. My Dad was far from a genius but it's a nice thought to end the chapter on.

Chapter 22

Battered by the barracks

My Dad had quite a few friends in Derry, ones he knew from school. One October night he, Stinker and a few old friends were getting ready at Seamus McKinley's house for a Halloween dance taking place in the nearby community hall in Bellaghy. Derry was without doubt a dangerous spot during the Troubles. Tensions were rife between Nationalist and Loyalist communities and the army had a heavy presence there. The Republicans refer to the region by its original Irish name or even 'Free Derry'. Loyalists call the region 'Londonderry'.

There's still some remnants of bitterness between the two factions on what it ought to be called. Just get a passionate Republican or steadfast Loyalist and sit them together at a table and ask them "Derry or Londonderry?" and watch the sparks fly. Even when I was growing up in the 90s I heard stories of boys in the year above me getting beaten up cause on nights out gangs of lads would just surround them and ask that very question. If you answered Derry you were a Catholic. Londonderry, you were a Protestant.

The simple facts are these: During the Ulster plantation by English and Scottish settlers, a new walled city was built across the River Foyle by a consortium associated with the companies of the City of London. In recognition of the London investors, the 1613 charter stated "That the said city or town of Derry, for ever hereafter be and shall be named and called the city of Londonderry." For Republicans and Catholics, the name is a constant reminder of how their lands were so recklessly taken from them. I personally could not give a shit. Call it 'The Mighty Kingdom of Her Majesty's Royal City of Londonderry' for all I care. I do find it quite humorous that on the BBC News when they're doing the weather they have to have 'Derry-Londonderry' on the prompter and in Northern Ireland train stations it comes up on the electronic banner 'Now approaching Derry-Londonderry'.

What does the government think is going to happen? That if you call it one name or the other that a Catholic or Protestant is going to fire a bottle at their TV screen or start a riot on the train? The lads chilled for about an hour at Seamus' and had a few cans. His Granny and Grandad had called in, as they were just about to head for a night out themselves and she popped her head into the living room. "Right boys, have a good night. But don't go around stirring any trouble. Just keep to yourselves and have a good time." There was going to be a congregation of both Catholics and Protestants at this dance and so his grandmother thought wise to heed the boys with a proper warning. "And if a bunch of Huns do start on you, aim hard and aim low" Seamus' Grandad shouted in "For fuck's sake, Andy would ye catch yourself on?" The grandmother scoffed at him. "Don't listen to that gobshite. Just go out there and try and keep the politics out of it. Love you, son" she said as she and the Grandad walked out of the house. "Love you, Granny" Seamus shouted back.

Huns was another nickname Republicans had for Loyalists. The Huns were a nomadic tribe from Central Asia that conquered much of the West of Europe in the 4th Century. They had great military prowess and even the mighty Roman Empire feared them for they were such a force. Quite the history lesson in this chapter, hey? In more modern times, the nickname tends to be reserved to describe Rangers supporters by Celtic fans. "Oh look, we play the Huns in the cup this week" or "we travel to the Huns on Sunday" was a common phrase that is still circulated among supporters. I remember being slightly bewildered watching Disney's Mulan when I was about 7 or 8. The soldier comes bounding up the steps of the royal palace and sinks to his knees in front of the Emperor "The Huns have invaded China!" "Jeez!" I thought "They're doing well for themselves." Now I do laugh when I think of how a child's mind works. Imagine thinking the two were in any way connected. The sight of a bunch of Scottish lads on horseback, bounding over the Great Wall in their Rangers' tops, with a sword in one hand and waving a Union flag in the other.

Dad and the lads set out and made their way to the dance venue and walked inside. It was a modest setting, but the organisers had done a good job. There was a local folk band playing on centre stage and a buffet table had been arranged so people could just grab and go, to the right was the bar and out back a few chairs had been set up in the smoking area. The lads found a spare table and settled down and just shot the breeze, Seamus was complaining about having to work with his Dad on the site. "The man has me running like a fucking dog. Fetch the pipes. Give that cord to your man. Get the cement bags shifted. It's non-stop." "Be grateful you have the work" my Dad chirped up. "Especially with a name like Seamus" During the Troubles the ratio to Protestants in employed work compared to Catholics was dire.

There were entire factories where you'd be lucky to have a single Catholic working in the joint. They were discriminated against to an unfair degree by the authorities and I'm not just saying that because I'm Irish and was born and raised Catholic. I studied arguably Northern Ireland's most famous poet Seamus Heaney for my English Lit. A- Level and in one of his poems he writes about how he's driving home after meeting up with a girl and is pulled over by a police officer. The officer asks his name and he replies with Seamus. The officer looks up from his notepad "Seamus?" he replies, in an almost accusatory tone, like being called Seamus was a crime in itself. The poem ends with Seamus being taken down to the police station and brought in for questioning about why he was driving the roads so late at night.

Something tells me he wouldn't have been brought in if he had responded with a name like 'Edward' or 'Henry.' "Right lads, my round" my Dad said and he made his way up to the bar. He was leaning at the bar and taking in his surroundings. There was a girl to his left who was standing between what looked like two farmers. You can usually tell who farmers are from a mile off. Patterned shirt, collar up and all wearing the same kind of boots. He made eye contact with her and she gave a brief smile before looking away again. Later that night he was on his way to the toilets and they passed one another, again she looked up at him and rather shyly glanced away. My Dad was like me when he was younger, rather shy, not sure how to go about approaching women, but drink does wonderous things, that good old inhibition destroyer.

Later that night the band was in full swing and both boys and girls were up on the floor jiving away. Right, time to bite the bullet. He got up from the table and brushed through the crowd towards where she was sitting. The two farmers had barely left her side all night, like bodyguards or trained dogs. He came up to her and leant in near her. "Don't suppose you could show a lad how to dance without looking like an eejit." He turned and pointed towards two guys on the dancefloor "A bit like him" and pointed towards a guy whose head was bobbing like a damn harbour buoy, "or him" and pointed towards a lad shimmying with a girl like someone had just stuck a cockroach in his pants.

The girl laughed "Oh, I'm not much better, I'll tell you that." My Dad smiled "Then we can make asses of ourselves together." She stood up, "Sure, why not?" She made her way up from the table and away from her two friends, who Dad told me were burning holes in him with their stare the entire time. I was talking to my mate Paul a year or so ago and we said we wished the whole boy meeting girl process was as simple as that these days.

Nearly all of my relatives: older aunts and uncles, Granny and Grandad met at local dances like this. The music would start playing and the men would simply ask women whether they would like a dance. Even if they weren't interested in them they would more than often say yes, cause it was simply considered the polite and respectful thing to do. If they hit it off they would date for a while and next thing you know it was an engagement, marriage and a family of their own.

Nowadays if you were to approach a girl and asked if she'd be interested in coming up to the dancefloor, their mate would probably record you and you'd end up on a video on Instagram with the caption 'Hate when creeps hit on me and my mates in the club.' So Dad and this girl made their way onto the floor and the boogeying began "I didn't catch your name sorry?" my Dad shouted over the din "Courtney" she smiled back. They swayed about for a while amongst the crowd. Now the McNamee men are no dancers. My Dad said he was a bit shapeless and to be fair I'd plant my flag in the ground with that statement cause I'm the exact same. One St. Mary's night out, I was with a girl on the dancefloor and there was traditional Irish music playing. She was absolutely nailing an elaborate Irish dance routine, she clearly studied it. I tried to respond with something similar and looked akin to a horse trying to buck its way out of a stable.

She beckoned me towards her and whispered to me "Fuck me, you really can't dance!" After a few more songs the two departed from the dancefloor and continued their conversation. Courtney's farmer friends had disappeared somewhere and Stinker was nowhere to be seen. The two decided to step outside for a breather, as they were making their way down the steps, a crowd of about 8 lads, including the two farmers were waiting for them. They all looked pissed. "Right, Courtney. Night's over, come on." He took her by the hand. "Uck, leave us alone Andrew. I'm not going yet." "Come on tae' fuck. We're meeting your brother down by the station." She wrenched her arm away "I said I'm staying."

He took a step towards her, then my Dad intervened "jog on, mate. She's not going with you." The lads circled in "Who the fuck are you anyway?" he asked "Charlie" my Dad said back "Catholic?" he immediately questioned. "Aye, I am". Wrong answer. The guy gritted his teeth and shoved my Dad back, "Yeah? Well, we're not so fuck off before I knock your teeth in." There was an army barracks about 200 yards down the road. They sprouted up all across communities in Northern Ireland during the Troubles.

This one was being patrolled by two soldiers who were observing the situation but didn't really flicker as the men closed in on my Dad. "Is that you, Mac?" a voice came from across the street. It was Stinker. He came running across the road, with a bag of crisps in his hand. He walked up to my Dad. "What's going on here?" he asked as the sea of angry faces glared back at him. "Best to clear out, Stinker. I'm about to get my head kicked in." "Really?" he said back. He then threw his crisps to the ground and called out "Right, which one of you cunts wants it first?" He turned around and nailed Andrew's mate with a hook to the jaw. The group stormed them.

My Dad said he landed one of them with a headbutt to the nose and caught another in the side of his mouth but they were soon overpowered and as the blows and kicks rained in, my Dad said he could hear laughing coming from the barracks. Soldiers during the Troubles weren't really concerned about keeping the peace amongst the locals. As long as rocks or petrol bombs weren't being thrown in their direction they couldn't care less. Hell, if they heard it was two Catholics getting pummelled they probably would have handed each of the guys a baton, or joined in themselves.

The whole incident landed my Dad and Stinker in hospital for a night but they were discharged the next day. As for Courtney, my Dad would actually continue seeing her. They dated for a while and she had two children from a previous marriage whom my Dad cared for like they were his own. She eventually became his fiancée, but unfortunately cancer struck and she passed away before they could get married. Her family never warmed to my Dad and after she died they took custody of the children immediately and he never saw them again. He had lost his future wife and two children he adored within the space of a month. Life sure knows how to kick a man when he's down.

Chapter 23

Meeting Mum

Colette Brogan was born in the year 1960. Her mother was Doreen McNally and her father was Joseph (Josie) Brogan. She had 7 siblings. Her brothers: Joe, Bernard, Paul, Martin and James, and her sisters: Kate and Anne. They lived at, in a two-storey house that was directly beside the grave yard and a stone's throw from the parish chapel where my Grandad worked as the sacristy. He tended to the maintenance of the chapel and graveyard and worked closely with the local priests when it came to such holy services as daily mass, weddings and funerals.

Therefore, as you would expect, it was a strict Catholic household that my Mum was raised in. But it didn't come from my Grandad's side. He was a holy man, yes, but a man of few words. He didn't rule his home with an iron, biblical fist and was more focused on the simple pleasures of tending to his garden or greenhouse than making sure religion ruled every aspect of his kids' lives and harshly lashing out punishments if they deviated from the strict moral codes of Catholicism. That was Granny's domain.

I imagine one of the reasons my Granny was so strict with my mum, aunts and uncles was partly because she was simply passing on how she was brought up. Her mother, my great Granny, was, as nearly all 19th/early 20th century Irish mothers were, rooted in tradition. Women were expected to keep everything in order in terms of theirs, their husbands and their children's livelihoods. That usually consisted of course of cooking, cleaning and naturally, disciplining their children.

I haven't heard many stories about my great Granny but I do remember Granny telling me once that my mum and Anne were coming downstairs for a night out at the Bridge Bar, Granny was sitting in the living room with her mother and as the two young girls entered, a scowl spread out across my great Granny's face. "And where are they going?!" she seethed towards Granny, "and with all that skin showing!" "Just up to the Bridge bar" my Granny replied. "Their brothers are all already up there". "Girls shouldn't be in pubs!" her mother snapped. Granny, therefore was always going to be a rather rigid disciplinarian.

Another factor was that her brother: Albert McNally, is a priest, although I think he's all but retired now, and her sister: my great Aunt Eithne is also a tremendously holy woman. Therefore the social pressure was likely immense. Dunloy was, and still is a very religiously tight rural community, but the problem with tight communities and small villages like Dunloy, is that everybody knows everybody's business.

Nowadays if your child is a little terror, or a bit of a rebel, most would probably laugh. "There goes such and such's daughter/son. Just like their mum/dad." But back then, whispers would manifest and people would harshly judge the parents, particularly the mother, if their child turned out to be a renegade, add in the multitude of holy religious connections stemming from every root of Granny's family and you're going to end up as my Mum did, living in a very regimented household.

Not to sound bias but I think Granny and Grandad did a damn good job raising my Mum. To me, she was nothing short of a saint. Devoted to her career as a nurse, where she worked long hours as nurses do. 8am to 8pm. I remember someone telling me a story at her funeral of how she stayed behind after 8pm to wash and style a patient's hair who was so gravely ill she could barely move. She then, after marrying my Dad would come home to 5 screaming children. She was run off her feet nearly all of the time. Never a moment did she have to herself, and things became doubly hard when Dad was diagnosed with leukaemia when I was 4 in 1999 and became so ill throughout his treatment he was bed-ridden most days. Even when he was well, my Dad was not easy to live with. He was a prominent gambler, on horses and football, and still smoked weed right up until I think he had to stop smoking altogether in his late 50s. He could be crabbit and prone to lose his temper.

Growing up I heard many an argument ensue between the pair. I remember some days she would flee to Granny's as an almost safe haven. Just to get away from it all. I remember once when I was younger, being with her at my Granny's. She was so exhausted she just sat back in the chair, closed her eyes and said "Sometimes I feel like just running away." She obviously didn't mean literally. She would never in a million years abandon her children, and if she ever was to leave my Dad, she'd be taking us along with her. I think she just meant she wanted to escape from the sheer workload she was having to take on. There are couples nowadays who wouldn't even fathom raising a single child together, but here my Mum was basically raising 5 of us, on her own.

The oldest, my sister Claire was born in 1990, and the youngest, Maria, was born in 1998. So there was a stage when she was having to handle getting us all up for school, washing us, dressing us, leaving us off, then making sure my Dad was OK, groceries, cleaning, calling round to her mother, picking us up, making dinner for everyone, homeworks, parents' evenings, bills, clothes ready for the next day, keeping us entertained, fallouts, tantrums, and arguments with my Dad. And this was all on her days off! I remember the 5 of us sitting around together shortly after she died and Claire and Aine just said. "How the hell did she do it?"

The Playboys were regulars up at the Bridge in those days. I remember my mate Tommy Kelly's mum Suzy saying that her and her sister Linda were up there nearly every other week with a baying crowd to watch them play. I imagine the primary reason they were so popular amongst the young folk of Dunloy was because they offered a window to a world that didn't really exist in the rural communities of Ireland, a world where you could let your hair down and just go wild, drink, have a bit of craic and party the night away. I also believe they most likely offered an aural relief from the music they were used to hearing back home; choir songs about our Lord and tunes so solemn you couldn't even make out what the singer was saying.

I don't think my Mum or Dad ever told me how they first came to be introduced to one another, all I know is that it was at the Bridge. My Mum did joke that the first thing she noticed about my Dad was his set of gleaming white teeth, which were mostly fake because when he was just over thirty he was helping a mate do some job that involved him being high up a ladder, as he was coming down he slipped on the rung below him and fell jaw first on top of the rung at the very bottom, which shattered most of his teeth. Mum, playing on this, said that on their first date she said. "I just have to say your teeth are really nice" she said my Dad then went, "Oh, thanks. Here have a closer look at them if ye like" and plucked them straight out of his mouth. The two came from very different worlds but growing up I noticed they always had the same cheeky sense of humour.

Meeting the parents is tough for any couple, but for Dad it must have felt like a baptism of fire. When I was growing up and he was on the phone to Stinker, every other word out of his mouth was "fuck". I wondered up until recently, whether he was just being deliberately crude, but a few months back I watched Dunloy FC play Strabane Athletic where my Dad's from down at the local pitch and the goalkeeper from Strabane must have shouted "Fuck!" about 80 times in the first half alone, I guess that's just the way around there. My Dad told me when he first met my Grandad he was so nervous and was trying to be a mixture of respectful and jovial but kept swearing after nearly every sentence and said to me he had to keep going "Sorry, sir".

He said my Grandad just sort of smiled and nodded, like he wasn't that upset, and that he appreciated that the man was trying to sharpen up and be respectful. I never heard about what his first conversation with my Granny was like but I could only imagine it would have been frosty and awkward as hell. She never was a massive fan of my Dad, she grew towards him a bit when he played in the chapel choir in his later years but I think she saw him as a bit of a renegade, and not a good suit for my mother, particularly given the fact that his job was unstable and he was never consistently bringing money into the household.

I remember one time after my Mum had went into the kitchen following a visit to my Granny after Dad had upset her one time, my Granny just shook her head and said to me "Your mother used to always say to me she'd marry a man who's long in pocket and short in breath, but instead she's done the exact opposite." Nevertheless, the two were a strong unit, they had to be, there was 7 of us at one stage crammed into a bungalow and you can count that 8 for a brief period when my niece Carly was born in 2009. They rotated roles well, when Dad was fit enough he would make the dinner, cut the grass and take us into town when Mum was working, and it was tough but they found a way. Love built a solid foundation for them. If the affection they had for one another wasn't as strong as it was our house would have swiftly collapsed under all the strain.

Chapter 24

A Glass Shave

The Playboys were on the road again, back to Scotland to tour a host of local venues right at the heart of Glasgow. Dad had now been seeing my Mum for just under a year, and they were saving up for their own place in Dunloy. It was nice that my Dad had something more tangible to strive for and motivate him in his work. Before he met my Mum it was just all about where and when he was going to get the next pint.

I mentioned briefly before that my Dad had developed into an alcoholic during his time with the band. He always was fond of the drink as he was growing up in Strabane but travelling with the Playboys accelerated the rate of his addiction significantly. They were constantly knocking back beers; after practice, whilst travelling in the back of the van together, just before a gig, just after a gig and of course basically the whole night. Such was the degree to which he drunk that his body could just circulate the copious amounts of alcohol he was consuming without even affecting his performance on stage. He told me that before going on he would down a whole bottle of vodka like it was orange juice.

He was never going to be able to sustain this lifestyle whilst keeping things in harmony with his family and his loved ones, and things did come to a head one night. His mother was appalled by his drinking problem, and whilst staying with her he said he heard rattling coming from the kitchen downstairs. He went to investigate and he witnessed his Mum with all of his beer cans and several bottles of vodka and she was pouring them down the sink. He yelled at her to stop but she wouldn't listen, he then went over to her and attempted to snatch the bottles out of her hand and as she poured the last remains away he told me he had his hands on her throat. That he told me was one of the most crystallising moments of his life. He knew then that things had spiralled radically and that he needed to seek urgent help.

With the help of his Mum they came across a rehab clinic, its name I can not recall but he told me that it was run by nuns. He said he hated every moment he was in there and wanted to leave right away. Everything was regimented, and he didn't like that one bit. You were told what time to get up, when to eat breakfast and they watched you like a hawk during all meal times. You were only allowed the bare minimum in terms of possessions and you were each assigned daily chores to complete such as mopping the floors and cleaning out the kitchen. It was like a mixture between a boarding school and a prison. You also had to have regular meetings as a group with one of the sisters, and Dad said he hated the way they spoke to you.

They always used an incredibly patronising tone and had a big goofy smile on their face, like they were pitying you. They were probably thrilled with the situation all these men found themselves in because then they got to do the Lord's work; guiding a herd of straying sheep back to the flock of salvation. "That fucking progression tree" my Dad said. Every week they would all sit in a big circle and there would be a large scale drawing of a tree on one of the chalkboards up front and sitting on a table would be a small bit of paper with each of their names, and some Sellotape sitting just to the side. Each one of them then had to come up to the front and place their name where they though they belonged on this "tree of progression", if you placed yourself near the foot; you were struggling, around the middle branches; you were making progress and at the top; then you believed you were more or less cured.

When it was my Dad's turn in his very first meeting he just slapped his name at the very top. "Oh, Charlie. You've put your name at the top of the tree?" Sister Anne queried "Yep." He said. "At the very top." "Now, Charlie" she said in a sing song voice, like a mother gently correcting their toddler for making a mess of their dinner. "Alcohol is a devilish addiction, time is a necessity when it comes to banishing its grip from within you. Patience and prayer is what is required to rid you of its curse." My Dad sat back down, folded his arms and rolled his eyes. He always had a fiery temper and going clean sober was only going to add to his propensity to fly off the handle, but he resisted. The way he saw it, the old critters were just trying to help, even though they were at times unbearably condescending.

He was in there for just short of 4 months, and the personal hell he endured in there was more than enough of a deterrent from looking towards the drink again. As far as I know he never touched the stuff after that. I remember him telling me about 6 years or so ago, just before my sister Claire got married that on her wedding day he would have a pint of Guinness as a toast to her marriage but he never did.

So the Playboys landed off the boat in Scotland one afternoon and decided to see the sights of Glasgow, the primary ones being the row of pubs that were in parallel lines all across the city centre. The rest of the band drank. Friel being the sensible one and the manager of course drank in moderation, the band members had quite a few, Stinker could drink for Ireland and my Dad nestled a Coca Cola. Later that evening they arrived at the 'The Sailor's Quarter' which was about a stone's throw from the harbour and pitched up their gear for the night. There were only a few locals to begin with but at around 7ish or so the crowds began to flock.

My Dad said they were a rowdy bunch, Glaswegians always are, and as they were setting up Dad said he had to keep leaning in to get wind of what Friel and the other band members were telling him to do over the cacophony of jeers, hoots and whistles. So once they got all set up, they began to play and the crowd appeared receptive.

They played a lot of folk songs because the Scottish tend to like something jovial that they clap along and stamp their feet to. "The Fields of Athenry" is a renowned Irish folk ballad. The song is a symbol of Irish culture and has incredibly poignant lyrics that reflect the strength of the Irish people's resilience. Some though interpret the song as a show of defiance against the British. The context of the song is set during the Great Famine and is about a man stealing bread to feed his starving family and is subsequently punished. In the lyrics include the verses:

"Against the famine and the crown,

I rebelled, they cut me down"

So a lot of passionate Loyalists would see it as being akin to a rebel song, which I think is bollocks but some people get sensitive about that sort of thing, and one of them just happened to be sitting in the front row when my Dad struck up the chords to it and began to play. He said he made it to about the 4th or 5th verse when a man stood up just a few metres away, eyeballing my Dad with his pint glass clenched in his hand. He launched the glass at my Dad and it shattered on his throat.

Dad felt the blood coarse around the tips of his fingers as he let go of the guitar head to clutch at his throat. There was an eruption of yells and the man made his way to the back of the bar and burst out the door, 4 lads gave chase and dashed after him up the road. The bar man threw a towel up on stage and Tiernan pressed it up against my Dad's throat. He was sat down gently on one of the chairs and an ambulance was rung. Dad got lucky-very lucky. He was told by the doctor a few inches to the left and his jugular would have been severed and it would have been lights out.

The group of lads who chased after the man caught him and he was handed in to the police. He served a 9 month sentence and had to pay my Mum and Dad £2,000 in damages as part of his probation, which he did in instalments cause he wasn't exactly loaded. It was a harrowing and traumatising experience for Dad but there were a few silver linings in the debacle. He was alive, and he and Mum were one step closer to securing a home in Dunloy, starting a family and hopefully settling down to a less hectic (although not that less hectic when we came along) life than the one he had experienced with the Playboys.

Chapter 25
Just a Blow-in

I would describe Dunloy as a very tranquil, quaint and pleasant little place to live, in my eyes it is the ideal location to raise a family. Nearly all the villagers know each other because they were all raised together in the very same parish, and so their children become good friends like they were, they attend school and play Gaelic and Hurling together and roam about the streets freely and without fear. I wasn't alive during the Troubles so I can't vouch for what Dunloy was like then but obviously there were tensions, and the villagers had a hatred for the British establishment that was bred into them from birth.

I remember Granny saying that one time Granda had to run out their front door and calm a local man down because right outside their gate he was squaring off and arguing with a British soldier. She didn't recall what it was about but she said from her front door she could hear him shouting "Shoot me then, you dirty fucker! Go on ahead and shoot me!" An argument could be made that the man had more balls than brains. You don't piss of a man holding a rifle when you're unarmed, especially when he could just shoot you dead and pull a Bloody Sunday and claim he saw you reaching into your pocket, or that you were a suspected member of the IRA.

The people of Dunloy are probably amongst the most passionate Irish patriots you'll find in Northern Ireland. Some still consider soccer a "foreign sport" and we didn't even have our own soccer team until Dunloy FC was established in 2008. My Dad used to coach an underage soccer team in Strabane and shortly after moving to Dunloy he came up to Eamon, who's my Mum's brother-in-law and asked "Who would I speak to if I wanted to start up a wee football team here in Dunloy?" "Soccer?!" Eamon asked with widened eyes "Yeah, is there anybody I could go to, to sort it out?" Eamon just laughed in his face, "Charlie, you must be joking." That sort of cavalier attitude still exists today, and is what grinds me a bit about Dunloy.

Some of the people can get very antsy if you show yourself as not being 100% invested in the Irish cause. My late aunt Anne ran a chippy in Dunloy. One day she went to open up and saw a giant tricolour hanging from the edges of the chippy's walls. "I'm not having that" she thought. "My business is open to everyone." She removed the flag and later that evening the chippy received a very aggressive phone call. It was from a local woman, where she was issuing out all sorts of threats and abuse down the phone at my aunt.

Anne just went "Uh-huh, yep, OK" then hung up the phone. "1-4-7-1" which is the number you ring to see where your last call came from. If the woman had chosen to select the 'withhold number option', she never would have been found out. But she didn't. Again, the old adage 'more balls than brains' comes to mind. The woman's number was read back out, my aunt scribbled it down and Anne rang the police, informing them of the number and once that was passed on, they located her address and paid her a little visit.

Dunloy is a village very much rooted in tradition, and to go against the flow is to almost automatically be branded as "unusual" or "weird". I was never massively into Gaelic or Hurling, I literally couldn't hit the ball on the ground with a stick to save my life and I only played Gaelic up until U16 level cause I just didn't have the strength, endurance or stamina to cut it with the big boys. There was one time a few years back I came into the VI to watch a county hurling match. The place was bouncing and guys were whooping, yelling and staggering about. I stayed till half time but wasn't feeling it so I left. Apparently one of the locals said to Chunk "That Tommy boy's an odd one isn't he?" to which Chunk snapped back with "You have no idea what that lad's been through so just shut your fucking mouth!" Deciding not to drink hasn't made things any easier to engage in the banter or revelry that goes on in the VI and Bridge bars.

One Saturday night recently my mate Oisin was over visiting from Australia with his girlfriend and we landed up at the Bridge. Every single person that we ever grew up alongside, went to school, played sport or partied with was there that night, it was unbelievable. Everyone was falling into each other's arms, absolutely hammered and I just looked at the clock as it hit 12.30am and was thinking "I've never wanted a pint more than I do right now." I imagine my Dad endured a similar struggle when he officially moved to Dunloy, off the drink and trying to assimilate into an environment that's whole social dynamic centralised around beer and hurling, a sport he had never seen played out until my Mum took him to a game alongside a few of her friends one afternoon to see Dunloy play in the Senior Antrim championship.

My Dad drove the lot of them up to Belfast for the big game. Alongside my Mum was her friend Grainne and her husband Phil. My Dad said Phil was a lovely, soft spoken fellow. He came across as quite shy, and spent most of the journey just staring out the window. Dad said he was telling them all of these crazy experiences he had when touring with the Playboys in Belfast. Getting stopped by the army every couple of kilometres to have the band van checked, and playing duck and cover when they left certain spots cause they were getting that many stones thrown at them. He also did a bit of stone-throwing himself up there back in the day, at army tanks after Bloody Sunday.

His close friend's nephew who was 16 was one of the innocents killed and so he felt a strong desire to retaliate in some fashion. He said when he was telling him all of these things Phil just chuckled awkwardly. I'm guessing Phil had led a relatively sheltered life in direct contrast to my Dad, if you stick to your own in Dunloy, nothing startling or dangerous is going to happen to you, but at the same time, nothing too eventful either, so he probably didn't know how to react to what he was hearing.

When they arrived in Belfast my Dad made sure to pick a spot that was public, but not surrounding too many of the estates or street corners. It wasn't uncommon for people to have their cars broken into when a big match was going on. It was easy pickings for hooligans as all the police and security are operating just outside the stadium and all the car owners are inside. People from Dunloy have told me that often back then as soon as you got out of your car, a youth in a hood would approach you and say if you paid him a tenner, he and his mates would guard your car to stop that from happening. You were then almost compelled to do so because if you just said to them "No, it's fine", they'd probably be the ones to do it.

When they got into the stadium, Phil said he wanted to stand right up at the front, whilst his wife was more keen to take to the stands near the back where there were seats. It was agreed that Mum would go to the seats with Grainne and Dad would stand up front with Phil. Eventually the game got underway. My Dad said the sound of the roars from the Dunloy crowd was deafening, and that Phil was amongst the loudest. Cursing and shrieking, calling the ref this and that and yelling at the Burr players, saying they were a "shower of bastards." Dad noticed as the game progressed that Phil was getting more and more agitated, his face had gone bright pink, and he was twitching and grunting with a big scowl on his face. What happened to the shy lad in the car an hour ago? There's something about the GAA that unlocks something within local folk; an almost primal, animalistic nature that is nearly completely concealed when they just go about their ordinary everyday lives.

I was doing a ten mile walk back in May and as I was chatting to two lads, this big hulking man came up beside us, pushing his young daughter in a pram. He was playing with her and smiling and cooing away. He knew Matthew who I was speaking to and he introduced himself to all of us, shaking our hands. He looked us all in the eye with a big smile on his face and was asking us all about where we're from, what we did and was joining in on all the banter. After chatting to us for a while he leant over towards his daughter and went "Come on, time to catch up with Mummy". He then said farewell to all of us and took off towards the front of the pack. "He's a lovely fella" I said to Matthew. "Aye, he really is" Matthew replied. "You know he came on for 5 minutes for Cushendall against us in the hurling and steamrolled two of our players and broke a stick he went in so hard for a 50-50?"

So the sport could definitely be regarded as a channel for unleashing any pent up rage. It also didn't help matters that Dunloy were losing the game and after the referee gave another- what Phil deemed soft call against Dunloy, he'd had enough. He let out a roar and tore down towards the front of the barrier where the security fencing was. He then tried to heave himself up and over the railing to get at the ref and my Dad just stood there, flabbergasted.

Phil kept attempting to pull himself up, again and again until my Dad eventually shouted "Jesus, man what are you doing?! It's only a game after all!" Phil then swung his head back towards my Dad, with fire in his eyes and bellowed "You wouldn't understand, Mac! You're just a blow- in!" A blow-in is basically a term used to describe anybody that integrates into the community, who wasn't born and raised there. There's couples who have been married and lived in Dunloy 30+ years but because the man's from Rasharkin or the woman's from Loughuile they're still blow-ins.

After that rather insensitive retort my Dad just thought "I'm not seeing the game out till the end with this nutter" and so exited the stadium and entered a bar just next door till the game's conclusion. Whilst he was in there he said he spotted a priest, sitting in a zipped up coat but with his clerical collar still on show, and he was necking a pint. Dad said he thought he spotted a betting docket in his hand as well. So much for the strict regulations of the priesthood. After the final whistle blew he met up with Mum and the other two and they headed back home.

The car journey was awfully quiet. Dad was pissed with Phil, and Phil was pissed with the result. He'd probably be brewing over it for the next 2 weeks. When my Mum and Dad arrived back at the house she asked him "Well, Charlie, what did you think of that then?" My Dad said "Never again will I be watching Dunloy play with a crowd of them ones. Sweet Jesus I've seen monkeys in the zoo less bat-shit mad than them."

Chapter 26

My Childhood

I was born on the 5th October 1995 in Ballymoney. I am the only boy with all 4 of my siblings being girls. We spent our entire childhood in a small one-floor bungalow located at 11 Bellaghy Park in Dunloy, which is located in County Antrim. There were 3 bedrooms in the house, meaning I had to share with two of my sisters; Rosie and Maria till I hit the age of around 13. It was quite cramped and what added to the pandemonium was the fact that at one stage we had 4 cats and 3 dogs. My Mum adored animals. So…14 living beings, all situated within the proximity of a tiny bungalow in the country.

Despite day to day life being hectic, it never felt like the dynamic of the house descended into utter chaos. Mum had established an effective routine, she never missed a beat, apart from the one time she forgot to put a horse bet on for my Dad when she went into town. She came home to find him dancing around the house with delight because he thought he'd just won £100, only for her to have to break it to him that she forgot to put the bet on. He didn't speak to her for 2 days.

On school days we were up at around 8am, fed, washed, dressed and at the gates of the primary school before 9. I was speaking to a few friends recently when we were discussing family meal times. Most people tend to have dinner between 5.30-7pm, or their evening tea as they like to say in England. We had ours much earlier. The steam was basically rising from the plates, freshly made when we landed in the door from school at just after 3pm. I think the reason for that was the sooner we were fed, the sooner we could be shifted out the door and spend the rest of the afternoon running around with our friends in their gardens or playing 40-40 by the kerbs and lampposts of the park. We as kids were very fortunate growing up in the Bellaghy district because nearly every home had children similar to our age in them.

There were the McPolands, Kellys, McAuleys, Dobbins, Kearns, Scotts, Rodgers, Weirs and Elliots. All within about half a mile each other. When we were running about you'd think there was some sort of flash mob forming the streets were that packed. I think what made things easier for Mum and Dad was that we were never overly unruly or spoilt children, yes we had our arguments and occasionally got physical with one another, but we were easily tamed. Mum once told me that on the weekends, the only way she ever got any housework done was that she stuck on 'The Singing Kettle', our favourite childhood show and all 5 of us would sat glued to the TV screen whilst she did the never-ending pile of laundry or scooted about the home with the hoover.

Another thing that kept us in line, was that when we overstepped the mark, we did get clashed. A lot of people think physical discipline is outmoded, and borders on child abuse because a grown adult should never strike a child but honestly, it never did us any harm. A clip around the back of the ear or across the head was simply a way of saying "No more!" All of our neighbours instilled obedience into our kids in the same way. My mate Oisin who lived next door said to me that one time he really didn't like the dinner his Mum had made, so he went to the bathroom and scraped all of it into the bin, his Mum just walked into the living room shortly afterwards and said. "I found your dinner in the bin. Your Da's getting towl when he gets home." and the colour just left his face. Trying to raise a kid in this generation must be hell.

Every incident is susceptible to being misconstrued or warped so that no matter what, the kid is the victim. I know that sounds cynical but I heard a story from a taxi driver that his mate's brother had a 15 year old who was a real renegade. He was getting up to all sorts on the streets, vandalising and charging about the town, doing as he pleased. One day he and his mates went and burnt out a bloody local community bus! When news of the incident reached the boy's father, he turned to him and said "I swear if you do anything like that again, I'll knock your head off." The boy then turned to his Dad and said "Do THAT!, and I'll ring social services!" The same principle applies in schools.

I have many friends whom are teachers, and I've worked as a classroom assistant since 2021. The paradigm used to be, the teacher dictates how well the pupil is doing. If they say there are not cutting the mustard, then their word is law. Now everything is open for debate, and teachers are scrutinised more now than they ever were. It used to be if a parent was told "your child is lacking in work ethic, they are misbehaving and it is affecting their grades. Improvement is needed." The parent would turn to the child and say "Buck your ideas up, and do what the teacher says." Now parents are questioning "How is my angel not scoring top marks? What are YOU doing to facilitate the needs of my child?", and their child could be the worst behaved pupil in the entire school.

We were very much outdoors kids. Me and my friend Ruairi did become very fond of the PlayStation when it was released in 1999, but usually the routine was, if it's raining, play away, as soon as it stops, it's off and you're out the door. I remember one time it was lashing out of the heavens, and so my mate Ruairi hit the power button on his PlayStation. The start screen hadn't even loaded up when the rain all of a sudden stopped and his Mum just barked "Out!"

Dad had been ill virtually my entire childhood. He was diagnosed with leukaemia when I was about 4, and was eventually told it was terminal. The crazy thing is, I had no idea how gravely ill he was. All I knew was that he was bed-ridden most days and that it was a rarity to see him out of his room. I don't think anybody but my Mum could have kept the 5 of us so obliviously unaware to the fact that Dad was slowly dying.

I remember every Sunday, maybe an hour or so after mass, Mum would just come into the living room with a very cheery voice, and say to me and my sister Maria. "Alright, get your Lego bricks gathered up! The priest's coming around to visit." We would then eagerly stumble about the house, gathering up our bricks and toys and firing them into the giant bucket. When Fr. MacGurnnigan came round, my Mum would greet him and lead him into Dad's room, she would then close the door and warn us not to enter, because they were having a "private" chat.

He was in fact, conducting the Last Rites ceremony for my Dad, because they didn't know if he was going to be around the following weekend. The Last Rites is a tradition in the Catholic faith, where priests will typically offer communion to the person who is on the brink of death, and allow them to reconcile and make peace with God before they pass on. Of course, by some sheer miracle, he would go on to live for another 20 years. He told me just how lucky he was a few years ago, when he showed me the letter he received from a medical clinic, asking him to come in for examining because they wanted to do studies on him to basically discover how the hell he was still standing.

He explained to me how he and 7 other terminally ill cancer patients were accepted to take part in an experimental treatment programme to see if they could find any way of staving off the cancer's progression. All 7 of the people who did the trial with him sadly passed long before he did.

There are many things that have happened to me in my life that I am deeply resentful about, but the fact I still had a Dad when I hit the age of 25 is something I will be eternally grateful for. It meant I got to hear all of the crazy stories that I'm writing about right now, which have provided me with some heartwarming smiles and deep belly laughs that I will always cherish.

Chapter 27

Dunloy on the 12th

On the 12th July 1690 the forces of William III; a Protestant Dutch prince and James II: a deposed Catholic English king met near the River Boyne in Ireland to contest for the sovereignty of the Emerald Isle. It was a pivotal conflict as William's decisive victory solidified the predominately protestant monarchy in England, Scotland and Ireland that exists till this day. In other words; the Protestants beat the Catholics, and here in Northern Ireland, the Catholics are never allowed to forget it, especially on the 12th. Every year the Orange Order organises bonfires and band marches that take place up and down the country to commemorate his victory. I think I heard someone say once that they are a homage to William as following his victory bonfires were lit to both welcome and guide him.

According to the Order, the core values of "Orangeism" which the bonfires and marches represent, include the promotion of the Protestant faith, maintaining the union between Great Britain and Northern Ireland, carrying out service to the Crown and delivering for the community. However, many members of the predominantly Catholic nationalist community, and some from Protestant and unionist backgrounds, say they view Orange marches as triumphalist and provocative.

I'm open minded about the whole issue and try not to let my Irish roots sway me too much in this argument. I believe if you want to celebrate the union that exists between Northern Ireland and England as a British citizen that lives in Northern Ireland that's fine. Light your bonfires and host your band marches. A lot of people see it as a community day, a family day, and a festive celebration during the summer time. However, I also wholeheartedly agree that a lot of these so called 'expressions of culture' are deliberately antagonistic towards those of Irish or Catholic heritage, and in certain communities, are publicised to a degree that flaunts, and almost teases Catholics in a blatantly sectarian fashion, or as I sometimes call it, giving a massive middle finger to all the Irish that still call Northern Ireland home.

The reason I say this, is because on a lot of bonfires, you will see being stacked upon them- a series of tricolour flags; the national flag of Ireland, and on some occasions, effigies of high profile Catholic figures, like the Pope for example. I was in Italy last summer over the period of the 12th (thank Christ for that) but on my Facebook newsfeed I saw a post that just encapsulates how hatred is being bred into generation after generation of youngsters in this country when it comes to political and religious divisions.

The post said 'Bonfire all ready for tonight. Thanks to everyone who contributed.' and there was a picture of a bonfire sat in the middle of a local park, during the day with a gigantic tricolour draped over it. Right next to it, you can see a bouncy castle, blow-up toys and a face painting pavilion, with a lot of kids who looked no older than 6 or 7 running about. I don't understand why such hatred is normalised in Northern Ireland. For me, it sets a terrible precedent for those kids. 'Look, children. We're burning the flag of a country cause we don't agree with its people or like to associate with them. It's fine.' It does go both ways.

I worked as a classroom assistant in Dalriada high school in Ballymoney for a year, it's a predominately Protestant school and I was the only guy from Dunloy working there. One day, I got a lift in with 3 other lads from Dunloy. They all worked as classroom assistants, at my old school; Our Lady of Lourdes high school, also situated in Ballymoney which is a Catholic post-primary institution. I hadn't told the lads where I was working, but when we came to just outside Dalriada, I asked them to stop so I could jump out. "Where are you going?" Anthony asked. "Sure I work in here at Dalriada".

As I clambered out of the car they all started shouting and jeering. "Why would you not come work with us?! Away te fuck! Ye dirty traitor!" Of course it was just banter but the attitude of Us vs Them exists throughout the country. When I was applying to teaching colleges I sent applications to both St. Mary's and Stranmillis in Belfast. When I told my Granny she just said, "Stranmillis?! Why would you want to go there? It's for Protestants!" When I saw that Facebook post in Italy I just shook my head, and showed it to my English and American colleagues who were working on the same programme as me.

They were flabbergasted. "Wait", one of the American girls asked "Why are they burning the flag of Ireland when they are living in the country of Ireland?" Irish politics is a shit show, and no-one really outside of the country knows a lot about its history, cause it's not at the forefront of the curriculum in schools. Callum; my brother-in-law who's from Manchester said he wasn't aware of just how fractured the country was, until he studied a module on Irish history for his History degree. It is quite funny at times the level of naivety present when it comes to people trying to understand how our country operates.

There's a famous American YouTuber called iShowSpeed who likes to visit a host of different countries and explore their cultures and traditions. He came to Ireland, and was walking about the north with an Ireland national football jersey on. He approaches 3 women sitting outside a café and asks "can you teach me some Irish words? Like "it's a beautiful day" or "I'm having a wonderful time in Ireland?" One of the girls responds:

"You're not in the Republic, you're in Northern Ireland".

"What?"

"You're not in the Republic- oh never mind…"

He then opens his arms out wide and looks around him. "What are you talking about?! We're in Ireland!"

In Dunloy, I'm sure they all wish the people of the country had the same mentality as him. Before the bands were prohibited from marching through Dunloy, I think it was around 2008 or so- most likely because the council decided the amount of time, effort, and money the whole event cost as it had to be so heavily policed just wasn't worth it, the atmosphere around Dunloy used to be like the calm before a storm. "You're not to be going up through the village this afternoon you hear me?" My Mum would say every year. "Why?" "Cause it's trouble." It was true, that tribal, primal nature I was talking about that comes out of the people whenever it comes to Gaelic games was very much thriving in Dunloy when the men used to come marching through with their big black bowler hats and orange sashes. My Dad told me that Powder Kearns, who lives just two houses down from us, rang our door one year with a hurling stick in his hand. My Dad answered the door.

"Let's get the bastards!"

My Dad came along, not to stir up the tensions but just out of curiosity. He loved a good show and sure he wasn't exactly the most steadfast of Irish Catholics. This is the man who sang 'God Save the Queen' in a Rangers supporters club in Glasgow for 2 bottles of vodka, remember? When he arrived, nearly the whole community had lined up on each side of the street where the band was marching through. The police were out in force, attempting to form a barrier between the marchers and the riled up villagers. Many still succeeded in getting onto the road.

My cousin BJ came out, clothed head to toe in Celtic gear with his long green and white scarf and sat cross-legged in the middle of the road, like a Republican Budha. One of the Pappys, along with other villagers who took their cars, parked a massive JCB truck smack bang in the centre of the road that the band was supposed to be marching through. If you search up Dunloy on Wikipedia you will see a small sub-section labelled 'Controversy over the 12th' that details some of the domestic scuffles that have taken place. My sister Aine showed me an entry someone hade made onto the Wikipedia page that has since been removed. I don't know if the mode still exists, but any user used to be able to edit and post entries onto Wikipedia. Someone had written:

'Did anyone see the shape of that absolute heifer that had to be dragged off the road by about 4 police officers? LOL'

I was in stitches. Someone verified later to me who it was. She was a rather large woman in the community, and each officer had to take an arm and a leg each and basically roll her like a boulder off the road. She was apparently shouting. "Tiocfaidh ár lá! Beidh Eire saor!" (Our day will come! Ireland will be free!) I think the best thing you can do to defuse tensions is have a good laugh, and by God I did some laughing at that.

Chapter 28

It's a Beautiful Day?

Dad did continue to perform, whether that be on the guitar, bass or keyboards after settling down in Dunloy. No crazy rock 'n' roll gigs though, those days were long behind him as his body couldn't withstand any long distance travel following his cancer treatment, but he would turn out for weddings, funerals, neighbour's parties or barbecues and showband competitions with a crowd of local players from Dunloy. One day, his old manager Friel rang him up. The Playboys had long since dispersed, but Friel wanted them all back together to do a wedding for an American friend of his who came to see the Playboys play a few times back in the day, and asked if they would consider playing at his daughter's wedding.

Friel rang round and asked them all would they consider doing one more show and they all said why not? It would be good to have the gang all together again. Stinker was invited too as roadie, although by this stage he was well out of shape; about 40lbs heavier than he was back in the 80s, and he was big back then. He also continued to smoke and drink to excess, like he did in his youth. He even still dabbled with the old nose powder, despite him being near the age of a pensioner. One Christmas he rang my Dad to check in on how we were all getting on. "Not so bad." My Dad said, "How's all of you?". "Well, Charlie. It might not be snowing but we're having a 'white' Christmas here that's for sure."

The day of the wedding came, and all of the men landed at the venue. It was a beautiful hotel in Donegal. Some considerable effort had been taken to make the place look like a fairytale wonderland. There were shimmering ornaments everywhere, and colourful banners and gleaming white pieces of furniture were placed all around the greenery outside. Inside, the staff were busying themselves; prepping the tables and even polishing the aisle, all ready for the blushing bride.

As they made their way in a tall, thin fellow, sporting a traditional gentleman's top hat and fully kitted out in his bold, black tux came striding towards the group. He extended his hand to Friel. "Welcome, gentlemen!" he bellowed. "So glad you could make it for this special occasion." "The place is looking great" Friel said as he took a glance around him to absorb all of the showpieces. "You've really pulled out all of the stops here." "Ah yes", the man replied with a cat-like grin, "a drab affair for my darling little girl." After he shook hands with all the band, they began to get set- up.

As my Dad was adjusting the microphones, he looked up and was startled by this woman who had just suddenly appeared in front of him. She was clearly the bride, sporting all white and wearing a whole host of make-up, and she was anything but little. She introduced herself. "Hi, I'm Audrey. The bride. I just wanted to ask if you could start playing 'Beautiful Day' (the song by U2) about a minute or so before I emerge from the entrance? I want to be coming up the aisle just as the chorus kicks in."

My Dad was confused. "Beautiful Day? We've not been told anything about playing Beautiful Day." The bride's face fell "But my Daddy told you all that he wanted you to play 'Beautiful Day' for me coming up the aisle!" "I promise you, I was never told" my Dad replied. The bride's eyes started to fill with tears and her face started to distort. "Well, he definitely told me that he said to your boss that you're supposed to play Beautiful Day!" Dad says that she was like a child throwing a tantrum after they were told they weren't getting any sweets from the shop.

It turns out that the father had said to Friel he wanted 'Beautiful Day' played. Friel said that would be no problem. "But the dickhead," my Dad said to me as he was recalling the story "Didn't even bother to pass on to us that we were to learn the fucking song." Dad said he kept trying to console her but she kept acting up. "But I asked for Beautiful Day! I want you to play Beautiful Day!" My Dad was starting to get pissed. He said in a firm but fair tone. "Listen, love. We're the band and we know what we're doing. Just trust us, we'll play a lovely song and it'll be great."

One of the bridesmaids, who was watching this all unfold, and my Dad said was about the size of Stinker, raised her hand and pointed one of her big sausages at my Dad's face. "Do I detect an attitude from you, sir?" she said in an accusatory tone. My Dad upgraded from pissed to angry. "Listen, go and get yourselves ready. We'll play a song we know. We don't know Beautiful Day. We haven't learned Beautiful Day. End of." The bride stormed off in a huff, and her friend went waddling after her.

The rest of the band had caught wind of the whole incident. Fergus came up to Dad and puffed out his cheeks. "God, she's a lively one", which was probably the kindest way to describe her. Tiernan then shouted over to them as he was wiring up the amps. "Just like Friel not to fill us in on what song we're supposed to be playing. We go on in just over an hour. Did he think we could just pull it out of our arses with no practice or what?" They began deliberating on what would be a fitting song for a bridal march when Friel emerged from the hotel lobby.

He looked rather stern in contrast to his usually warm and cheerfully receptive disposition. He beckoned the band towards him with his hand, like the team captain calling a huddle before a big game with his players. Stinker was at the bar chatting to two of the guests with a pint in his hand. He's not usually the most swift or efficient but when he saw there was a bar he got all of his gear set up in double-quick time. Friel clicked his fingers at him and pointed towards the rest of them. Stinker came sauntering over and Friel leaned in with a furrowed brow. "Right, who's went and upset the bride? Her Dad's just told me one of youse has left her in tears back there." His eyes were wrongly fixed on Stinker, cause if there ever was someone who liked to put his foot in it, it was Stinker. He had a habit of just blurting out what he felt.

He could be standing in front of a local fishmonger, or the president of Ireland and he'd still be incredibly loud and uncouth. One day me and my mates were in our house and Stinker was over visiting my Dad. He walked straight up to the three of us and just went to Ruairi and Oisin. "So where are you two from?" "We just live next door." Ruairi replied. "Is that the house with the red and white painting on the door frame." "Yes", Ruairi replied. "Our Dad painted that." "Tell him he's done a shite job", he remarked and just walked on. For a while Stinker lived in a very Loyalist part of Belfast.

He was the only Catholic living there. There were Union and Ulster flags on every pole. One day, just outside his house he was leaning up against the lamppost, fixing his shoe. "Well, Liam?" one of the locals shouted over. "What are you at today?" "I'm just about to scale this pole and wipe my arse with that coloured toilet paper hanging up there", he casually proclaimed. Decorum and an awareness of his surroundings just isn't a part of Stinker's psyche.

So if anyone was going to upset a bride on her special day, it would be him. "What the fuck are you looking at me for?!" he clapped back. "Wasn't even anywhere near her, though I could hear the bloody banshee crying and caterwauling from back at the bar." "Well, whoever did it should be ashamed. We're here to do a professional job." Dad stepped in. "And how are we supposed to carry out that professional job when you didn't even let us know what song we're meant to be playing." Friel looked startled. "But sure that's what I was just coming in to tell you. 'Beautiful Day' by U2. Sure everybody knows it. "

"We friggin' don't!" Tiernan blurted out. "Oh shit", Friel replied meekly. He always liked to believe he was above swearing, but he was starting to panic. "Well, come on. Think. What's a good song for a beautiful bride to walk down the aisle to?" "And one we can all play?" Fergus chimed in. "How about that song? It's a traditional Irish jig", Stinker suggested. "#She is handsome, she is pretty, she is the belle of Belfast City#. Brave and easy song to play too". "We're hardly going to call that diva 'handsome' on her wedding day." Tiernan remarked. "She'll have our throats". They continued to deliberate for another few minutes when Dad had a sudden lightbulb moment. "Howl on a second chaps. I think I've got the perfect song to have her walk down to."

The congregation had all shuffled into their seats. Final words were being had with the priest conducting the ceremony and through the glass pane window of the hotel lobby doors, the bridesmaids could be seen mustering themselves into position. The song the boys had decided on playing was to take place after the official declaration of the marriage, when the bride and her husband were walking back down the aisle. The traditional wedding bridal theme chimed in, and the wedding was underway. Dad and the rest of them were on standby. Once the priest had announced "You may kiss the bride." All of the guys were in position. Charlie nodded at his backing players behind him and stepped over the microphone. The music kicked in and dad began to sang.

#Isn't she Lovely- Isn't she Wonderful- Isn't she Precious...#

The song they had chosen was. 'Isn't she Lovely' by Stevie Wonder. Dad said all the guests were cheering and clapping, and the bride had the widest of grins on her face. "Make it all about her." He said to me when he was telling me about it. "All eyes on me, aren't I wonderful? And you'll not go wrong."

At the reception, later in the night, Dad and Stinker were sitting at a table with a crowd of Americans. They always seem to have quite a profound fondness for the Irish. My old colleague Shauna said the routine usually goes when you travel to America, cause it happened to her and two of her friends, is as follows:

"Oh my God! I love your accent. Where are you from?"

"Ireland"

"No way! You know I'm 1/14th Irish on my Grandfather's side?"

So they were just shooting the breeze, when all of a sudden the topic of leprechauns came up. Stinker when pressed on whether they were real said to them. "Oh yes, they are real. Charlie killed one of them." "Wait! What?!" one of the girls cried out. Stinker turned to my Dad and gave him the universal signal to play along. "Yeah, I did. I was driving home late one night from a gig, and one of the wee fuckers just jumped out in front of me, so I ended up ploughing into him with my car." "Didn't you stop?" One of them asked. "To see if they were OK?" "Nah", my Dad said without fuss. "I just drove on." "Murderer!" The hysterical girl cried out. "How do you sleep at night?!"

I'm not saying Americans are stupid, but by God they can be gullible. Which was the exact word my mate Dean used to describe them after he spent a year there for uni. If you say anything with conviction, 9/10 they will believe you. I proved this theory true when I was participating in the AngloVille programme last summer in Italy. I met two American girls; sisters from Brooklyn. As part of our cultural exchange programme with the kids. Each mentor had to give a 5 minute presentation on the history and culture of their country. Me and Connor, who's from Clare, were hosting our presentation on Ireland.

We discovered that the national animal of Ireland was the hare. One of the sisters then put up her hand. "Wait, I thought the national animal of Ireland was the leprechaun?" I then said. "No, leprechauns are mythological." Two seconds later her sister responded with "Hold on, are leprechauns real?" The story of my Dad's encounter with the Americans flashed through my mind. I had to do it. "Yeah, they are real, and they are humans. But they have really tiny brains, are only about a foot tall, and all they do is steal, which is why in legend they're known for having a pot of gold.

My Dad actually killed one. He was driving home from a gig late one night, and one of them jumped out in front of his car, once he hit it, he was concerned, but upon discovering it was just a leprechaun, he drove on. Cause they're horrible little creatures." Her mouth was gaping open. She then said. "But a human being is still a human!" Lord have mercy. They also found it quite confusing when we announced the time. If we told them it was 8.15am and then 35 minutes later they asked us the time again, "It's ten to." We'd say. "Ten to what?" was the response we'd get. Connor also told me he knew a girl from America who was half Irish, cause her Dad was from Cork. A group of their friends were sitting together, and when they met each other for the first time she asked. "Do they have hospitals in Ireland?" I said to him, "You should have said no. We conduct open heart surgery with shears on the side of the road next to the cows and sheep…"

God Bless America.

A Journey of Troubles

Chapter 29

The trip to Pissnaskea

As you can imagine, as a family of 7. We didn't venture out on too many holidays together. The holiday to Lisnaskea in 2004 was the only trip we went on together as an entire family. The only other holiday I have ever been on with both my Mum and Dad, was a week in a caravan in Scotland. My two oldest sisters; Claire and Aine were exempt from this trip. They were teenagers and far too cool for a leisurely family getaway, instead they stayed home and threw a massive house party with all their mates which I don't think Mum or Dad ever found out about. Dad wasn't fond of travelling. He didn't enjoy life on the road when he was with the Playboys. "Cramped up in the back of a musty van, eating bags of Tayto cheese 'n' onion crisps. Then getting prodded out of the band van at gunpoint by the army at every fucking checkpoint."

He never had a passport, never needed one. He only travelled there and back to England on a plane twice in his life; to watch a Premier League game with me in 2012, and for my sister Claire's wedding. I think the thing that irked my Dad so much about travelling, and in particular family holidays, is the stress. I was talking to a man up at the Bridge a few months back and he said that holidays are no longer holidays whenever you become a parent. "I just took my two kids away on holiday for the first time there in January and I fucking hated it. Never again." You see it all the time.

Whenever I've been in airports there's always families with kids that are throwing tantrums. "Buy me that! But I want it now!" Then the poor Mums and Dads are sitting in the waiting area by the flight announcements and their kids are ducking and weaving in between strangers and they have to go galloping after them. Whenever the kids become teenagers I think things change, they're more independent and don't need to be constantly guarded.

When I went to Lake Garda with several families from Dunloy, we were all 15, 16, 17, and so the parents would have a BBQ or head to a local bar whilst the seven of us went off and explored. Dad's short fuse also tended to exacerbate matters, like when we got lost getting off the ferry in Scotland. We arrived at night, at about 8pm and were driving around in the dark for about 40 minutes looking for the campsite. "Where the fuck is this place?!" my Dad seethed. "Says it's supposed to be on the second turnoff as soon as you exit the harbour!" My mum tried to calm him down. "Settle, Charlie. We'll find it. We'll find it."

What made things even worse is that he pulled up to a set of teenagers, lingering around a street corner with their hoods up and asked them for directions. They sent him the complete wrong direction, I'm guessing intentionally for a laugh because we had to do a complete 180 after my Mum rang the site and they pointed out where we should be. When we finally arrived, Dad just plunked himself down on the sofa and said. "I'm getting the first boat back home on Monday." He did stay it out for the week, but never left the caravan. He just sat watching horses and flicking through the teletext, which is exactly what he did at home.

For the trip to Lisnaskea, all of us kids were getting settled in the car to leave when Christopher Kearns; Powder's son from just down the road, appeared at the car door. He put his finger to his lips. "Shh" he said. "I'm coming too." He clambered into the open boot area, where all our luggage was and ducked down. We were all giggling. Christopher was always good for a laugh, but was flirting with the prospect of being viewed as a crude tearaway. He used to pass me on the street, when I was still in primary school and say. "There's Tommy Tucker the little fucker!" One day, all of us and our friends were playing about in the blow up pool in the back-yard. He then lifted our cat Poppy and just launched her into the pool as well.

She let out a fierce shriek and leapt out of the pool, covered in soapy suds. You'd be done for animal cruelty for that nowadays. So all of us, with Christopher bundled in the back, set sail up the road. We had drove about a mile and a half when Christopher popped up and starting singing "#We're all going on a summer holiday! Yes, we're all going on a summa' holiday!#

My Mum and Dad just laughed. "Out tae' fuck you!" she chortled, he leapt out of the car and began the walk back to Dunloy. "Are we not going to leave him home?" I asked. "Having him walk all the way back there on his own?" "Aw he'll be fine" my Mum laughed. "The eejit."

We had travelled a fair distance, and were getting close to Fermanagh when suddenly, a bird flew right onto our windscreen. We all screamed. "Fuck me!" my Dad yelled. "The wee bastard's gone straight into the window!" "Pull over, Charlie!" my Mum yelped. "I need to make sure it's alright." We pulled up and my Mum delicately lifted the bird off the car and placed it gently on the side of the road.

She used all of her nursing skills to care for the creature and attempt to revive it but it died. That was typical of my Mum, she just had this innate desire within her to care, whether that be human or animal. The death of the bird was an omen of things to come.

We landed at our rented accommodation. It was a large house, a spacious one. Good for a big family. We all scattered about to explore. "Right, everyone." Mum called out. "Go and pick your rooms." Claire and Aine wanted to bunk together, cause they were the closest in age and so shot down to the end of the hall and ducked into the room on the left. Rosie, Maria and I took the room on the right. We had set all our bags down and were looking in the cupboards and through all the drawers when suddenly we heard Aine scream. "AHHH! OH MY GOD!" The three of us dashed down the hall and into their room. Claire and Aine were standing with their hands over their mouths and pointing to the corner.

There was a large, almost cocoon like structure with several craneflies, or "daddy-long legs" as we liked to call them, all buzzing about it. "I'm not sleeping in here!" Claire cried out. "Not a chance!" Dad had to go fetch a broom and dismantle the hive, but they still refused to sleep in there. Instead they just made make-shift beds out of the downstairs sofas. The kitchen wasn't in great nick either. The windows were besmudged with stains, and a lot of the cutlery that had been used by the previous occupants hadn't been washed. Not exactly a dream holiday thus far.

On top of that, it hadn't stopped raining from the moment we arrived. It wasn't a light drizzle either. It was heavy rain, absolutely bucketing and as we looked out the kitchen window, all we could see was the long stream of water, funnelling down the windows as we stared into the back garden. It was a fucking depressing sight. That's why in our household, our one and only family holiday together will forever be known as: the trip to Pissnaskea.

We had only booked to go away for the weekend. (Thank God), and on the second day Mum took us all to the local leisure centre pool. It was a large complex, with about 3 different large pools and a number of colourful slides. Me and Maria were the youngest, and couldn't swim so the slides were basically off limits to us. Claire, Aine and Rosie were playing away, whilst we were standing looking pretty miserable in the corner.

Then Mum had an idea. "Hey, how about you two go down the blue slide, and I'll stand at the bottom and catch you." We were well up for that. I went first. I barrelled down the slide and Mum scooped me up as I entered the water. As I was making my way to the side of the pool, a woman got chatting to my Mum and she was turned towards her speaking, facing away from the slide. Maria then came shooting down and plunged into the water. Mum hadn't noticed, and neither had any of us.

All I remember is a few moments later, Mum coming walking towards us, holding Maria's hand and she was crying. She had went under for about 4 or 5 seconds before Mum had noticed, and Mum had to haul her by her arm out of the pool. I'm trying to think if there were any happy family moments to highlight from that holiday, but there were none. It was a shitshow from start to finish. My sister Aine has two kids both aged 4 and 2, and has said to me she is never taking them away to a foreign country or to some resort. The stress and risk involved, just isn't worth it.

Chapter 30

Losing Uncle Bernard

My uncle Bernard Brogan was the baby of the Brogan family. He was thoroughly charismatic, always cheerful, and would always bring us around treats and gifts from his numerous travels. He was a bus driver for a very high end travel company, and transported a number of big showbiz names and celebrities to and from their hotels and venues whenever they fared over to our country. He lived in Claudy with his wife Bernie in a lovely, quaint bungalow- a bit like ours, that had a beautiful, spacious front garden that was decorated with an assortment of flowers that shimmered in the sunlight and made his home look almost fairy-tale like in its majesty. I think he got the gardening bug off my Grandad, cause he too was very dedicated in the maintenance and upkeep of a pristine setting of well refined greenery, to compliment and add to the visual appeal of the home.

It was a summer's evening in 2007. I had spent the day at my friend Daniel's house, and made my way back to ours. When I got into the living room my two sisters Rosie and Maria were staring at the TV with sullen expressions on their faces. I can remember 'Who wants to be a Millionaire?' was on the telly. Dad was over by the window, pacing up and down and gazing out the window as if he was looking intently for something. He clocked me entering the room. "It's your uncle Bernard, Tommy. He's had a heart attack and passed away in the hospital."

He then turned back towards the window and continued to stare out towards the direction of the road. "I ran the hospital (Causeway hospital, where Mum worked) to get them to pass on the news to her about an hour ago, and she's still not back yet. It was stupid of me, it'll have sent her head into a spin and maybe distracted her on them busy roads." Dad was a serial worrier. If somebody was late, something had gone wrong. Standing by that window in the living room was his personal worry spot.

Shortly after Aine had Carly she moved to the house just across the road. You could see into her driveway from that window. If there was ever a bit of snow, heavy pouring rain, or even if it was slightly gusty, and my sister's car wasn't in the drive. Dad would say: "Geez I don't know if I like the idea of Aine being out on them roads in that weather." I'm the exact same. I don't worry as much now but when I was younger, even up until a few years ago if somebody was 15-20 minutes late for an appointment and hadn't called or messaged me to inform them why they weren't there yet, I assumed something disastrous had happened.

I always remember my heart pounding when I was in primary school, and the ITV news came on the hour on evenings my Mum was working, cause I was just waiting for the presenter to say "There has been a heavy car collision on the M3 in Coleraine." And I'd just go. "That's Mum!". So Dad was pacing frantically for about 10 minutes when Mum's car came around the corner and she pulled into the drive. When she got out of the car, I could see her face was red and blotchy, and tears were streaming down her face. When she got into the house she was sobbing and my Dad hugged her. It turns out she had heard the news about uncle Bernard, but not from the staff at the hospital.

She had already left once she finished her shift before my Dad made the call to Causeway. She had heard when she was driving past my Granny's house after stopping into the Costcutters to lift Maria some Porky Pear lollies, to try and cool her down because she had been suffering from a temperature and saw the unusual amount of cars parked in my Granny's drive. In rural communities, if you see a swathe of cars parked along a road in somebody's park, on in their driveway, then somebody has passed. Word spreads fast throughout villages, and upon hearing the news locals all convene to pass on their condolences and comfort the members of the family the death most deeply affects. It was when she saw all of the cars and then went in to investigate that the news was broke to her.

We were all dressed in our finest, preparing for the drive down to Derry to attend Bernard's funeral. It was my first funeral and to me they are without doubt one of the worst mental trials you have to endure, I suppose that's stating the obvious. For me, wakes are worse, but we didn't attend the wake due to how far away Bernard's home was. I just hate everything about them.

The sea of black, the vacant expressions on the faces of those attending, the uncomfortable shuffling as you navigate in and out through various bodies, the awkward conversations you have with relatives or your friends with whom you shared a mutual connection with the person that has passed and the absolutely earth-shattering looks of devastation and defeat on the faces of the wife, husband, brother or sister whose loved one has died. I've attended a lot of funerals in my time. Too many, and it never gets any easier. I think one of the worst aspects of a funeral is having to see the loved ones of the deceased, sitting right at the front of the chapel. It's even worse in Dunloy.

In Dunloy's chapel, there isn't rows of benches all facing the same way towards the altar at the front, instead it's shaped like a large dome, and all the benches are arranged in a big circle, with the altar smack bang in the middle. That means everyone gets a front row seat to see just how broken the person's relatives are. I hate that. Then there's the readings. It's common in the Catholic church, I'm not sure if it's the case with all churches for multiple, not just one, of the person's relatives to conduct a short personal reading, at the podium, for everyone to see. Nearly every time this happens, somebody ends up breaking down and sobbing, barely able to get their words together and it's downright soul destroying. Then when the coffin is lifted and carried out of the chapel, everyone is in floods of tears. It's such a traumatic experience, particularly for a young person and I wouldn't wish anyone to have to go through what I did at such a young age, witnessing multiple funerals of close loved ones.

It mentally scarred me. I was grateful I didn't even get to go into the chapel, such was the vast amount of people in attendance, the day of my old school mate Eoin Henry's funeral. We were in the same year together at Our Lady of Lourdes. He was diagnosed with cancer around the age of 18 or 19, and died when he was 20. I can only imagine that within that building, as it would be for the funeral of any very young man or woman that passes away, that the atmosphere is a thousand times more solemn.

One of the worst things about somebody close to you dying is that for the majority of people that attend the funeral, life goes back to normal the second they hop into their car and leave the parish hall or the house where the tea and sandwiches are being served. "It's a pity" or "It's a shame" are usually the words that gets mumbled on the journey back. Then the topic of conversation changes to something decidedly more light-hearted. What also riles me up, is that some folk, particularly the older generation, revel in the sort of environment that sweeps in when someone dies. They love to talk about it, to speculate and weigh in on the situation.

Mum told me that Bernard's wife Bernie had gotten upset, because one of her neighbours at his wake came up to her and said: "Yes, I thought I noticed Bernard coughing quite a bit and holding his chest when he was doing his gardening the other day", and she responded by asking, "Do you not think you could have told me that?". Some people are so fucking braindead and downright insensitive. What good was it going to do Bernie by passing on that information? For our family in the weeks following the funeral, we did our best to move on, but Bernard's death absolutely shattered Mum. She wasn't her usual cheerful, effervescent self.

When she came home from work in the weeks following the funeral, she just went about her duties. There was no laughter lighting up our home, no wise-cracks with dad and no bubbly conversations. I remember she came home from the shops once, it was just a few days after Bernard had died, and she was annoyed. "I've just came from Sweet Home", she said. "And there were two older woman standing at the till with the shopkeeper, laughing away and having a grand time, and I felt like saying to them. Are you not aware that my brother's just died?" Sadly, that's the way the of the world. The earth doesn't stop spinning when someone you care about passes away, as I would come to learn myself. I remember going into my Mum's room one day, and she was crying quietly on the bed. I sat down beside her and said "When will you stop being sad, Mum? When will things go back to normal?" "They never will", was her response. "When someone dies, everything changes, and nothing is ever the same." I was going to discover, less than 4 years later, that truer words were never spoken.

Chapter 31

Along came Carly

Things were frenetic yet functional as usual in our home as I finished primary school and made my way to high school. Mum and Dad's aptitude for handling the ever shifting hormones of teenagers was put to the test, with my sisters Claire and Aine reaching their senior years at Loreto college, and with it all the pressures of assimilating into Irish social culture for girls, which mainly consisted of underage drinking and chasing boys. Claire always had a very mature look about her, even as a teenager. She was very tall and didn't wear excessive amounts of make-up. Her demeanour was very modest and the way she carried herself didn't give any off any inclinations that she was any younger than the age of 21. She told me that on Fridays when she got home from school, she would change into her most sensible looking clothes, 'borrow' my Mum's handbag and nip into the local off-licence. It's all about attitude and confidence. Some people would place underage drinkers immediately into the bracket of anti-social renegades. The type of people who get into fist fights and commit vandalism and petty theft.

In Ireland though, it's more like a rite of passage- a maturing process. Some of the most educated and responsible people I have ever met, people who have gone to the likes of Cambridge and become professors were bouncing off the walls at the ages of 15, 16, 17. I remember coming from Our Lady of Lourdes to do my A-Levels at Dalriada; a very high-achieving grammar school. I saw a framed photo on a wall in one of the corridors: 'Pupils achieving 10 or more A*-A grades at GCSE', and there were about 20 students standing in the photo. Everyone's uniform was so well maintained, and all the boys and girls were so respectable. "Hi there. Welcome to Dalriada. Would you like me to show you around the school?" "Yes, Miss," "Thank you, sir". Then one October, shortly before my 17th birthday on a Thursday night, I got a call from my buddy Ryan, who also made the jump with me to Dalriada Sixth Form from OLOL. "Tommy, you've got to get over here. This place is mad! It's fucking carnage! I've never seen anything like it." He was ringing me from the Bush Tavern in Ballymoney, where the Lower and Upper Sixth of Dalriada used to host their monthly 'socials.' "Give me 10 minutes. I'll be up now." My neighbour dropped me off in Ballymoney and when I walked into the bar…it was like something from the last days of Rome.

Dance music was blaring, strobe lights were flashing, people were lying sprawled out all over various sections of the bar and queues of students were lining up taking shot after shot. A girl who couldn't even make eye contact with me when I introduced myself to her in my first week came running up to me, eyes doing cartwheels, with a drink in her hand and threw her arms around me. "AHHHH! TOMMYYYYY!" So it really is something of a cultural norm.

My sister Aine was also a bit of a party animal in her youth. School never really suited her, and she didn't see eye to eye with a lot of the teachers at Loreto. Her and her friends used to hang out with a crowd of lads from Dunloy. Lads I all still know, and would chat away to cause they're sound blokes, but back in the day they were rowdy characters to say the least. When Aine hit the age of 15, she was going out more and more often, and having to be disciplined time and again. Alcohol only added to the fires of rebellion, and she was starting to get more unpredictable and impulsive.

Then one day, two friends of mine who were in my year that attended Loreto; Ruairi and Fearghal, took me to the side separately for a private chat. Rumours had been swirling about around the bus and within the school that Aine was pregnant. I was startled to say the least. At the age of 13, I didn't have the emotional capacity to process the news. Then one day, Mum took me for a walk. As we were heading towards the park she just said, very quickly, cooly, and with no dramatic build-up. "You know Aine? Well, she's pregnant." "Oh…" I said, surprised that the rumours were true. "Well…is she going to have an abortion?" Mum stopped walking and turned towards me.

I thought she was going to thump me. "Of course not!" I don't think Aine ever contemplated with the idea of having one. I've never asked her if she did. She's never been overly religious, so I don't think that the traditionally Christian 'all life is sacred' debate contributed to her decision, but seeing her now as a Mum of three, I've noticed she's taken after my mother in terms of being a naturally caring soul, who's whole focus of life evolves around providing for her kids. Dad wasn't half as composed about receiving the news as Mum was. For a solid month, the atmosphere in our home was toxic.

Dad was livid. Nearly everyday I'd come home and he'd be yelling about the issue towards Mum. Mum would yell something back and Aine would be caught in the crosshairs. My sister Rosie did a short documentary called 'Our Carly' for her btec media course, and Aine reveals that the weeks following the pregnancy announcement were a tumultuous time, and that Dad had said some particularly nasty things towards her. I remember Mum and Dad nearly separated because of it. Dad had to go stay with friends in Strabane for a few days in order to attempt to cool off, and Mum conceded to me that she didn't know if he'd be back.

When Carly arrived. Delivered on the 26th December 2009 at 12.03am, all of our lives changed dramatically…for the better. She had the roundest face, brightest blue eyes and most adorable smile I've ever seen. She was constantly cooing and laughing, and she injected her home with a spirit I hadn't seen since we were all youngsters toddling about the household. Dad adored her. There's one picture in our kitchen, and I've never seen Dad look as happy in his life. He's holding Carly up towards his face. Her, with a big, toothy grin, and him, with the broadest of smiles. "Where would we be without her?" he said in the kitchen one day as she was stumbling about. She wasn't even 1 when Mum was diagnosed with cancer. I'll never forget the look on her face when we were all sobbing in the living room after the news was broke to us. She looked so bewildered and confused. Mum attempted to rally us all together. "This is going to be tough." She said. "But we've got Carly, and she's going to be the ray of sunshine that gets us through this." In the months that were to follow, we'd need her shining light to lift us more than ever.

Chapter 32

The worst chapter of our lives

It was approaching the end of summer in 2010 when I noticed Mum complaining more and more about pains in her stomach. The first thing she dismissed it as was indigestion. However, as the weeks progressed, it was starting to interfere more and more with her daily routine. To manage our household required all hands to the pump, and having to stop and sit down quite often because of the pains she was experiencing was frustrating for her as she was the central pillar, the foundation of our household that kept things running, and brought everything and everyone together. Eventually she booked in an appointment to see her doctor.

I was sitting in the kitchen one afternoon doing my homework, and she was preparing dinner at the counter. "So how did the appointment go?" I asked. "They found an inflammation", she said calmly. The cogs of worry that were embedded within me since I was a boy began to work into overdrive. "Could it be cancer?" I immediately responded with. "I don't know", was her meek reply. "I have to go for further scans." Trying to distract myself in the lead up to that scan was an endeavour in itself. I did my best to throw myself into school work, friends and football, but every time in the house I would see her wince and clutch her stomach revived the burning question of "What if?". On the day of her scan results I was at school. Her meeting with the doctor was to take place in the afternoon, and she would be home shortly after we arrived back on the bus.

That school day I was present in body but not in spirit. I couldn't concentrate, not on work or interacting with my mates. It's only a 10 minute bus journey from Ballymoney to Dunloy but it felt like the longest of my life. When I arrived back at the house my aunt Anne was doing some ironing and sorting out our clothes. I took a seat by the window; Dad's old worry spot and tried to watch the TV but found myself glancing out the window every 5 seconds, just like Dad used to do, waiting for the family car to appear around the bend. About 20 minutes later the car appeared and pulled up into our drive. I caught Mum's face through the front car window and she just smiled at me. It wasn't a beaming smile. Looking back now I can tell it was a pained smile, like the kind you give out of courtesy when something devastating has happened to you and somebody shares their sympathy.

As they entered the house I could see into the hall from the living room but not the front door. Aine was standing there and as she looked at Mum and Dad her face just fell. She put her hand to her mouth. "No!" she cried out. Neither of them had said a word. Their faces must have just conveyed so much pain and angst that she was able to tell straight away that it was terrible news. Mum appeared into the living room, still maintaining a smile. "Come on into the living room everyone", she said. "It's OK." I immediately started to weep. Dad appeared around the corner and I have never seen a man look so utterly defeated.

All of us were gathered in the living room along with Anne. She was used to giving out bad news to families. She was a nurse and had did it many times before, but never to her own family, to her own kids. She had the most calm, professional demeanour and her eyes were dry as a bone. I probably reacted the worst out of everyone because in my eyes that was it, she was gone. I think for everyone else they saw it as, this is cancer. There's a strong possibility she could die.

But again for me, and I think for Dad as well because as everything was unfolding he just sat in complete silence, we were already trying to comprehend how the hell we were going to get by without her. Anne took me by the hand and told all of us that we needed to be strong for Mum. Mum too did her best to console me. She looked at me and continued to smile broadly. "Look at me, Tommy", she said. "I'm right here. I'm not going anywhere." If only that were true.

The next few months were like a blur. Bowel cancer is particularly aggressive so she had to start chemotherapy as soon as. Watching the effect it was having on her was traumatic in itself. To see someone who is normally so vibrant, and who always made the most out of life, no matter how challenging slowly fading, being drained of her energy and getting more frail everyday was a nightmare. I remember one day she took Rosie and Maria with her to go wig shopping once her hair started falling out. "We'll make a day of it!" she said cheerfully.

Even now she was still trying to keep the household full of positivity and she was doing her best to ensure the environment of our home didn't become corrupted by the constant scourge of cancer that sucks the life out of all families. She went for a check-up following her first round of treatment and the news wasn't good. The cancer had spread and was continuing to spread, rapidly.

One night she was lying in her bed, and was laughing and joking away with her sister Kate, her brother James and his wife Rita. A stream of guests had visited her that day, and I wanted to see what was up. When they left I walked into her room. I wanted to know there and then what was going on. "So your chemo." I mumbled. "When are you starting your next round?" Mum's face fell. She looked me straight in the eye. "I'm not", she uttered. "Well what does that mean?" I sharply replied. The room was dead silent for about 5 seconds. "What do you think it means?" My eyes started to well up and the first thing I did was walk to the end of the room and shut the door.

I didn't want Dad to see me cry. I then went back towards the bed and fell into Mum's arms. She held me close and began to brush her fingers through my hair. The composure she had shown throughout her diagnosis and treatment was gone, and she began to cry as well. "I remember", she said through her tears. "When you were just a toddler. You would constantly be crawling around at my feet when I was trying to hoover or do the dishes, and I would say: "Tommy for God's sake I need to get some work done here", and you would just look at me with them big blue eyes and say: "I'm sorry, Mammy. Please don't be mad at me." Dad opened the door and entered. He had the same desolate look on his face that he had the day we found out it was cancer. He just walked over to the bedroom window and began to gaze out. Like he was searching for something, not for a set of car lights to allay his worries this time, but for an answer to the question: Why? Mum continued to hold me close as she sobbed. "You know something?" she wept. "I'm not afraid to die…the only thing that kills me is that I won't get to see you and your sisters grow up." Those words are my inspiration in life. I find them to be so haunting, as they ring through my head every day yet beautiful.

My motivation to be a good man, a good person, is not fuelled by moral obligation or guilt through religion. It's them words alone. I don't believe in God. I can't comprehend why such cruelty in the world exists. It would be self-centred of me to say I don't believe in God or the Bible because of what has just happened to my family alone but death, destruction, war and famine that wrecks the lives of decent people is everywhere, and a lot of the time religion is the cause of it. I can tolerate religious people, as long as they don't shove their beliefs down people's throats which unfortunately a lot of Christians feel compelled to do. I also don't like the fact that a lot of them quote from a book that was written 3000 years ago to support a lot of outdated mindsets and justify heinous actions, and don't get me started on that whole "It's part of God's plan" bullshit.

When Mum was comforting me she said "You know my whole life has been about you and your sisters. Youse have always come first…especially over your Da" she smiled and glanced in his direction. He just chuckled as a brief smile spread across his face. "Oh, I know that." So it was confirmed there and then that Mum wasn't going to live much longer, and now a family of 7, which included a baby that had yet to turn 1, was going to have to somehow get by without the beacon of light that was my Mum to guide us through the messy maze of life.

Chapter 33

Goodbye to Mum

It was a Thursday morning when Mum passed. She had been admitted for hospice care just over a week before. I remember being awoken in the early hours of the morning by a frantic stirring from the hall. It was the sound of feet clambering across the floor, and eventually I heard the sound of Dad's voice saying "Let's go!", following by the door opening and closing. I went into the hall to investigate what the ruckus was about and my neighbour Dolores was waiting by the front door. "Come on over to your aunt Anne's", she said. "And try to get some rest. Your Mum's not well and your Dad and sisters have gone to see her in the hospital." Me and my youngest sister Maria ambled across the road to Anne's and as I lay down on her bed, I prayed that Mum wouldn't die. Not yet. Not before I got the chance to see her and say goodbye. Despite being fraught with worry, I managed to get over to sleep.

When I woke up a few hours later Dolores was sitting on the end of the bed. She had a sullen look on her face. "Tommy, I'm sorry to tell you but your Mum's passed." I was devastated. "But I didn't even get to say goodbye!" Dolores took me by the hand. "None of them did", she replied. "By the time they reached the hospital she had gone. I'm sorry." Claire, who was in the car with Dad on the way to hospital, said she was sure they were going to crash. "I looked at the dashboard and he was doing close to 100mph. I thought we were gonna have a collision on the motorway."

All of us gathered in Anne's living room. We were all just staring vacantly into space, a mixture of shocked and maybe slightly numbed. We knew this day was coming, but the hectic nature of the events that took place that morning still meant our minds were swirling, and we were a bit disorientated.

When Anne came in she just approached us one by one and kissed us on the forehead. She swore she would look over us and protect us when Mum passed, and she did. To alleviate the pressures of my Dad in our small bungalow both Aine with baby Carly, and Maria moved into Anne's house across the road. She was a magnificent guardian, and really drove us on in the years following Mum's death. Unfortunately she herself would pass away from a sudden heart attack just over 4 years later in 2015. Dad said at times he thought there was a curse placed on our family.

When someone passes away in an Irish community, especially if they're well known and respected like Mum was, your family has to brace themselves for a stern test of endurance. The process of making wake and funeral arrangements such as catering, moving chairs and tables, constant streams of visitors who want to speak to you personally and tell you what a great person your loved one was, organising readings, going through how the ceremony will pan out and trying your best to remain composed is thoroughly draining, both mentally and physically. I remember during the first few nights of the wake, you could barely manoeuvre around the house. It was just wall to wall with visitors.

Eventually it got so crowded that I was able to duck into my mate's house and chill there for an hour and a half before anyone noticed I was gone. The hardest part of a wake is without doubt, having to see your loved one's body resting in an open casket. The undertakers arrange for the body to be well presented and elegantly dressed, but when you look down into the coffin, it doesn't look like a person you're staring at. Dad told me that when he was a young boy, seeing a body at a wake for the first time traumatised him for years. Somebody his family knew had passed, and he said that despite displaying clear signs of trepidation, he was basically forced in the door, and made to stare down at the body to show his respect. I was the first out of the 5 of us to see our Mum in the coffin.

The girls couldn't face it just yet. They later said to me that I was very brave because whilst Father McNally was hosting a prayer ceremony in Mum's room, they all waited outside whist I took up a spot, right beside the coffin and just stared at Mum the whole time. No tears filled my eyes. I don't think my lip even quivered. I had done most of my grieving in two stages; when Mum told us she had cancer, and when she told me it was terminal. So I just stood there, stone-faced. Dad was much the same.

On the day of Mum's funeral we were all gathered in the living room, along with family and close friends as the priest and the undertakers began the process of raising the coffin, and bringing it out into the street. It usually begins with six or so men, lifting the coffin together and locked arm to arm, they help support one another and bear the weight of the coffin as it is carried to the chapel. If the house is a far distance away, the coffin is usually brought in the hearse but because our home was only about a mile or so from the chapel the decision was made to carry it through the streets.

It was both heartwarming and eerie to see the extent to which Dunloy had just frozen as my Mum was being brought out. Every single house up and down our park, and the surrounding parks had its residents standing at the front of their door, dead silent and heads bowed. If you had dropped a pin half a mile up the road we would have heard it. When it was my turn to help carry, I stood on the left of the coffin, Ruairi stood on the right, and we allowed the weight of it to come down on our shoulders as we made the slow and steady journey through the village.

No 15 year old should be carrying the body of their mother through the streets with their friend. Eventually we reached the chapel and shortly afterwards the ceremony began. Me and my sisters all did readings. Aine was reduced to tears as she finished hers, saying what a great nanny Mum had been for her daughter Carly Mae. I was relieved when Mum was finally laid to rest and we made our way into the parish hall for tea and sandwiches. I remember being in quite good spirits, laughing and joking with my friends. I've used humour all my life to defuse and de-escalate situations, and I was just so desperate to escape the atmosphere of depression and misery that had hung over my head like a cloud ever since Dolores had told me Mum had gone.

However, like I mentioned before, the hardest part of losing a loved one isn't the wake, or their funeral; times when everybody rallies around you and repeats the old adage "If you need anything, my door's always open.", then they disappear and you don't see them again for maybe 3 or 4 years, it's the period of adjusting to life without them, and we had a hell of a lot of adjusting to do. We were just lucky we had Anne to guide us. I was into my first GCSE year at the time and she helped me to stay motivated and keep on the right track. Maria was only 13, and of course Carly when Mum died had just turned 1, with Aine who was having to try and adjust to motherhood when she was still so young herself and now no longer had her own Mum to show her the way.

However, she managed to drag us through the roughest period of our lives, and therefore it's only fitting that this chapter concludes with a commemoration to her. She raised us well at a time when Dad was severely struggling. Her, along with my next door neighbour and best mates' mum Dolores, made sure we were never found without means of support, whether that be making sure we always had clean clothes and that 11 Bellaghy Park was in order, or letting us stay in their homes, which Dolores did for me when my house was being renovated by John Dobbin.

He was a very well to do contractor and he, along with a lot of local men under his employ, completely refurbished my bedroom and our kitchen, free of charge. That's one thing about Dunloy, I bash it all the time by saying how boring and uneventful it is, and how the infrastructure is terrible but its people are the beating heart of the community. They're hardworking, friendly and always come through when you need them. I can't even recall the numerous stories I've heard of guys doing jobs for free on a Saturday for their aunt or mate's granny, or local Mums who maybe already have 3 kids of their own taking in other families' children into their care for no charge if their parents are working or busy. If it wasn't for the support network that the people of the village provided during the toughest period of my life, I don't think myself, or we as a family would have got through those next few years.

Chapter 34
The Pompous Priest

Dad liked to keep himself occupied as much as possible, even when he was breaching 60 and should have been having thoughts of slowing down. He liked to be the man in charge when it came to cooking the dinner, and the kitchen was his domain. He very much liked taking the lead, and always had the mentality that if something should be done, it should be done right, which did grind on me at times. I didn't start learning to cook properly until after he passed away, cause every time I tried to do something basic like boil and egg or use the oven he would be hovering over me like a fly, making sure the temperature was adjusted correctly and warning me of just how long the intervals should be before checking in.

If any of my relatives came round and asked "Does Tommy cook any of the dinners?" He'd just say "Absolutely not! Don't want the bloody house burnt down!". It was the same for mowing the lawn. When I went to cut the grass he would just stand by his favourite spot at the living room window and glare out at me, cup of tea in hand. He would then knock on the window and make gestures if I missed a spot, or tell me to go over the same patch twice if I hadn't cut it straight enough the first time.

He would frequently take trips into town, and loved a good bet on the horses and football. I used to laugh because if he saw our neighbour John McAuley coming from down the road as he was watching the horses he would groan and say, "Fuck sake. Here comes John to put the scud (curse) on me." He said this because one time John came in and sat down in his room and nearly the second he did that, Dad's horse that was winning, fell at the next hurdle.

He knew quite a bit about betting since he had been doing if for so long and one year he won £2100 because he had bet on 4 teams to win their respective leagues; Chelsea, Wolves, Sheffield Utd and Hibernian, and they all did. Though he used to always piss me off on a Friday evening cause he would show me his betting docket for the weekend's fixtures, and every single time one of his bets would be the 12.30pm Saturday game. I always tell people. "Never bet on the early Saturday kick off because if your team loses then your entire weekend's finished."

He never listened to me, and I remember for about 7 or 8 weeks every Friday it was the same. "Take a look at that and tell me what you think." "Why the fuck are you betting on the early kick-off? If they lose your entire bet's done." He would just nod his head and put the docket back in his pocket, and I swear every single time his team either lost or drew, which he meant he had to go rush back into town at about 2.30pm to make another bet before the 3pm games.

He was a stubborn owl git. I mentioned previously that he still played in the chapel choir, local folk band contests and at weddings and funerals. One of his music partners, who he performed countless weddings with was a talented local singer called Christina. One day she landed at the house, to ask if Dad wouldn't mind doing a wedding with her in Kilrea. "Sure." Dad said. "No problem." Dad loved playing, he would play anywhere and at times would accept jobs when he was in no physical condition to do so. He also only charged £100 to play, which is insane given the prices you have to pay these day for any sort of showpiece band to play at your occasion.

At Ruairi's pre-wedding night out in Crumlin jail in Belfast, they had to fork out nearly £2000 for a band to play for around 2 hours or so. Dad made his 'extensive' preparations that involved getting me to look up the songs on YouTube and playing them over a few times by ear, no learning chords was needed at this stage, and he and Christina set off for Kilrea one Saturday morning.

They arrived at the chapel and got all their gear set up. The performance area was in a little cordoned off corner to the side, diagonal to the bottom of the aisle where the bride and groom would be entering from. They spent a short time going over the entrance hymn as the guests came streaming in. Everyone had taken their seats, and a lull descended over the chapel. That was their queue, or at least they thought it was. The band struck up and Christina had begun to sing the first verse when a cry of "STOP! STOP!" came from the top of the aisle.

The priest was there, fully kitted out in his ceremonial robes and came marching down the middle of the aisle. "I give the say-so on when we start! Not you!" Dad says most of the guests had turned behind their seats, and were watching this incredibly awkward spectacle unfold. "Sorry, Father." Christina replied meekly and he bounded up back the way he came. Dad said he thought she was going to burst out into tears. She made it through the procession, but Dad found her sitting in the car-park afterwards sobbing. The priest had made a complete show of her in front of a packed chapel. Time to have a word with him. Dad made his way back into the chapel and entered the priest's quarters. He told me he was sitting on an arm-chair, with his hands placed on both rests, like a regal king from the Tudor ages. Dad said he could tell just by looking at him that he was an arse-hole. He told me he had sovereign rings on each one of his fingers, and he was pointing and beckoning to the altar servers to fetch him things.

My Dad approached him. "Father, can I have a word?" "Who are you?", was his snappy response. "I'm one of the players from the band, and I just want to say you were bang out of order talking to Christina in that way. That girl has never hurt a being in her life, and you've really upset her." Dad said the priest just scoffed. "And what makes you think I care about what you have to say?" Dad's eyes widened. I said he had a fiery temper, and throughout his life he had to bite the bullet more than once but this time he couldn't hold it in. He took a step closer to the priest. "Here, Father. Why don't you do us all a favour? Get off your high horse, and come down to my level." The priest was aghast at the audacity of my Dad to speak to him in this way. Priests are basically royalty in the Catholic Church.

In years gone by, whenever they would do their rounds to local households after Sunday mass, the TV in the house would have to be switched off, and everyone would have to gather round to listen to his wonderful words. A bit like Jesus. Some priests probably though they were Jesus. The priest stood up from his chair. "Get out of my chapel! OUT NOW!" Dad said he just turned on his heels and marched out the door. He clambered into his car where Christina was sitting in the front waiting for him. "Where've you been, Charlie?" she asked. "I just had a wee word with the priest. Told him what I thought of him." Christina, like a lot of the community from Dunloy, was a very religiously devout woman, and was absolutely affronted. "Oh no, Charlie!" she cried. "You didn't! You shouldn't have!" "Yep, I did. Come on. Let's get out of here." Dad said he went to start the car when he looked in his wing mirror and saw the priest coming up the path towards him with two stocky men on either side of him, like two goons that were protecting the Godfather.

Dad said they were probably local boys. Part of the "GAA mafia", as he described them. Dad turned the engine on, put the throttle down and headed for the gate. The gate wasn't fully open, and as Dad accelerated through he knocked the right hand side off its hinges and he tore up the road. Christina was hysterical. Defaced the priest's reputation and chapel property. All in a day's work. "Oh, Charlie McNamee!" she screamed. "I'm never playing with you anywhere again!" I don't think she did after that. I don't see what all the fuss was about. Sure the priest could've just sold a few of them sovereign rings of his to repair the damage.

Chapter 35

The Gutter Cowboys

If you need any maintenance work done, whether that be paving, painting, construction or fittings. There'll always be someone in Dunloy that can lend a hand. Nearly every man in the village (not including myself), knows how to work his way around a set of tools. Minty McPoland next door is basically the DIY master of the park. He was one of the leading frontmen in constructing the garage in his back garden which acts as his own personal workshop. I've been in it a few times and it's basically a smorgasbord of wooden planks, tools, paint cans, measuring devices and worktops. Dunloy is a village packed with natural tradesmen. They usually go down that route because they grow up witnessing their fathers doing similar jobs, and they usually follow in their old boy's footsteps as they develop a passion for their trades at a young age.

Many a Saturday morning in The Bakery you'll see boys that look about 14 or 15 with their work trousers on that have about 6 pockets down each leg for their tools with their hands all black and crusty. For the majority of men in Dunloy, university isn't really seen as an appealing option, which I completely understand as a lot of them are skilled enough at what they do that they don't need a degree to make a stable living.

Nearly all of them, particularly in recent years, go to the local tech a few days a week when they're doing their apprenticeships. I think it's compulsory now that all upcoming workers have to log in a certain amount of hours learning theory such as safety protocols and grasping precise units of measurement so that their companies can tell the government that they have been officially trained, which a lot of the young lads I know are frustrated with and see it as more of a box-ticking process than of being of any value. My cousin Oisin McCamphill a few months ago was explaining how downright pointless he felt his university lectures were.

He's attending the University of Ulster in Jordanstown to do construction, with a particular focus on bricklaying. He said this lecturer was just standing at the podium talking about the different types of brick there are, and was taking them on a journey through Greek architecture and the way buildings were constructed back during the first civilisations. Oisin told me he and 6 other lads just got up and left whilst he was speaking. The way he explained it cracked me up. "How the hell is telling us about the kind of brick that was used for building about 4,000 years ago gonna help us when we're out trying to build a bloody wall?" I'm the polar opposite to most Dunloy boys. I find theory and essay writing far more enthralling than construction work of any description. I remember in year 8 I couldn't even make a decent photo holder. I messed it up twice and so Gerry the caretaker just banged one out for me over lunch one day.

I think I was also the only pupil in my class to get an 'E' in my technology test in year 10. It's hard to relate to the locals at times whether that be in the pub or at a match cause a lot of times they want to talk about their work such as what jobs they've been working on and the productivity of each of their companies and about how all the lads over at Dowds, NIE and Creagh are doing. This was epitomised for me one day when I was 17 and had been studying for my A-Levels close to summer. I came out to my front garden for a break and Anne was there supervising Paul McQuillan who was doing some pavement work for us on his hands and knees.

He looked up at me. "Who's this young fella?" "That's my nephew, Tommy. He's Collette and Charlie's young boy." Anne replied. Paul pulled a frown "Never seen him about. What does he do?" "Oh he's a studier this one. He's all into the books." Paul grimaced. "For fuck's sake! Get him doing some real work. Put a set of boots on him and a trowel in his hand!" I never liked receiving praise. I don't think there's an Irish man who does and with the men in my community in particular they never seem to praise other men, for anything.

An All-star hurler could walk into the local after scoring 2 goals and 11 points in a big game and whilst some would pat him in the back, there'd always be one or two who would just yell across the bar. "Ah, you're still shite! How did you miss that 45 in the second half?" I remember the day I got my A-Level results. I came in from the school with my results in hand, Dad was making his way from the kitchen to his bedroom with a cup of tea. "Well, how'd you get on?" "I got 2 A*s and an A". He just nodded. "Happy days, you're flying now. I'm just away back to bed here. I'm still wrecked." Nothing more needed to be said. He was happy, I was happy. Job done.

For a while we had been experiencing some problems with our gutters. They were old and eroded, and they were getting caked with dirt and a build-up of grime. Like I previously mentioned, there's always somebody in Dunloy good for a job, and so Anne recommended a group of local men she knew who would be fit for purpose. The three of them landed down one afternoon with all their gear. They knocked on the door and I answered. "Is this Charlie's place?" "Yeah it is." "We've just been sent to set up a new set of gutters. Alright if we get cracking?" "Aye, no bother."

So the men got to work and after about a week had installed a new set of white shimmering pipes that ran all around the perimeter of the house. It looked a good job, clean and fresh with solid structural integrity. But what did I know? One morning Dad came into the kitchen with a face of thunder. "Them bastards are worse than the gypsies! £700 they charged me for that job and look out the back here!" I followed him out the back and he pointed to the corners of the house where the drainage spots were.

Some of the gutters were lying crumpled on the ground, whilst some were swinging from the edge of the roof. "Nothing but a bunch of cowboys!" he seethed. That's the problem of employing local help instead of going through a legitimate company. There's no quality assurance guaranteed, no tracking process and of course, which enraged Dad. No refunds.

I was working away in the kitchen one night when a sheet of paper landed in front of me. Dad pointed to it. "Have a read at that. A wee project I've been working on." I looked at the sheet of paper. At the top was the title. "The Gutter Cowboys", and below it were the following lyrics:

#Well for a while I had been in a pickle

#For the water on my roof did trickle

#Then one day the cowboys came into town

#Promising to take away my gloomy frown

#They came and worked at my feet

#Highly recommended from a friend across the street

#But much to my surprise- the gutters they worked on all week round#

#Are now lying where they shot up from-flat bang on the ground#

Chorus:

#Life time job they told me- 10 year guarantee. Now £700 later. I'd have to disagree.

#Sure made a fool of me…

He brought me into his room and played it for me on the acoustic guitar. He had worked on his own chords and everything. What made it even funnier was that when he sang it, he put on a Southern American accent- just like a cowboy. He told me he wrote it in about 20 minutes which was quite impressive. John McAuley came in one evening and Dad played it for him. I could hear John laughing away from Dad's room. "That's actually good, Charlie", he chuckled. He brought his guitar up to my aunt Kate's one evening and played it for her and her husband Eamon.

He said Kate erupted into a fit of laughter and was out of breath she was laughing so hard. "Get into the Village Inn and get that song played, Charlie." Eamon grinned. "For those boys will be floating about in there." Anne wasn't too happy about the song. She knew the lads who did the job personally, and I guess she thought it was making a bit of a mockery of them and her judgement at the same time. He didn't go around playing it for the entire village, although he told me he was sorely tempted to. I guess he just needed a healthy way to vent his frustration, and writing a catchy tune seems like a better idea than most to me.

Chapter 36

Somehow still standing

As Dad was growing ever closer to 70 his energy did begin to wane, and he was finding it more and more difficult go about and enjoy the simple pleasures he thrived on such as trips into town and playing with the choir or for the parish at community events. In his later years the only time I saw the faithful guitar brandished: a guitar that still remains enshrined in his old bedroom, was when the McPoland's next door would have a BBQ and Dolores would ask me to call in on Dad to whip around and they'd all sit in a circle to listen to him play some classic Irish ditties that they'd merrily clap along to. He spent most of his days confined to his room, which he absolutely hated. He never liked the feeling of being trapped and that he wasn't in charge of what was going to happen to him next.

I remember Mum telling me that on the day of my 2nd birthday he was bed-ridden in hospital as an effect of the intensive chemo he was receiving for his leukaemia. He could barely walk. Then all of a sudden he threw over his bed covers, detached himself from the monitor, stood up and began to amble towards the door. "Charlie, where on earth do you think you're going?" The startled nurse blurted out. "It's my son's birthday today." Dad said with authority, "And there's no chance in hell I'm spending it in this hospital!". Though the fact was that at his age now, and with everything his body had been put through over the years whether that be drinking, smoking or cancer treatment, completing simple tasks such as mowing the lawn, going for grocery shops and being receptive to his friends and visitors that would check in on him on a regular basis was leaving him exhausted and at times disorientated.

One day, he came to me and my sisters and explained that he was experiencing a lingering pain in his throat, it hurt in particular when he swallowed. He was prescribed paracetamol yet the pain did not subside and after a few weeks he began to experience swelling in the lymph nodes on his neck. He had to go for a scan and the feeling of dread our family has had to experience time and again resurfaced once more, and once more our fears were confirmed; it was a tumour: a cancerous growth that had developed, and was growing rapidly. It had already started to affect Dad's speech. Treatment was needed, and fast.

After a consultation with the doctors it was decided that he would undergo external beam radiotherapy where high-energy beams are focused on the tumour from outside the body to target and destroy cancer cells while preserving surrounding healthy tissue. It was just me and Maria in the living room with a doctor who had came out to visit along with Dad who were all present to break the news. He obviously wanted a professional to lay down the facts as sensitively as possible because doing it himself just wasn't in his repertoire.

We were naturally shocked and deeply saddened but also hardened from our previous experience with Mum. Dad was just numb, almost to the point of detachment. I suppose a plain way of describing it would be like when you experience a dead arm or leg, and if somebody was to repeatedly keep striking it you wouldn't even feel the pain, such was the degree to which he had been left wearied and worn both throughout his life, and by the trauma of the last 10 years. He told me that if it wasn't for the five of us, and his granddaughter Carly, he would have just thrown in the towel and not bothered going through with the treatment.

Just over a week later my sister Aine left him into Causeway for his radiotherapy. When he arrived back home he had a massive bandage all up the left hand side of his neck. Dad looked like he'd just survived a missile strike, and when the bandage was removed the skin underneath was raw and red, as if someone had taken a flaming torch to it. In the weeks that followed he was even more trapped to the confines of his room. He was irritable and completely washed out. He was also getting more and more frail looking as all he could eat was soup, and even then he would have to swallow very consciously with him often wincing in pain as it travelled down his throat.

Eventually he regained some sense of himself as the months passed, and his strength returned to a degree when he was able to consume hearty portions of food. Dad's idea of an average meal I can safely say was substantially greater in terms of portion size than most households. My sister Claire will tell you herself that when she came to visit he would put on an entire bag of potatoes and a huge shepherd's pie along with carrots. When he set the plate down in front of you, swimming in gravy, it looked akin to something you'd try to devour as part of a contest to win a prize or discount at a restaurant. He had to keep going for regular check-ups but life returned to something resembling a state of normality, that was until he began to feel a tinge in his neck and the swollen sensation in his nodes came back.

A scan then confirmed it, the growth had returned. The whole aggravating rigmarole of appointments and meeting with consultants was thrust back into his life much to his dismay, and it was eventually decided that another round of radiotherapy was no longer a viable option. The only pathway now was surgery, if the procedure was deemed as not being too high risk.

I remember the day of Dad's meeting with the doctor to find out what decision they had reached. A consultation of leading professionals had been held prior, to weigh up whether it would be worth trying to remove the tumour given its proximity to Dad's artery and the potentially fatal outcome should something go wrong. I was in school on the day he found out, it parallels the day I had to endure in high school back in 2010 when I was waiting to get home to find out what the results of Mum's scans were.

The emotions were much the same; fear, angst, trepidation and the most nauseating butterflies in the pit of my stomach all through the day. When I pulled up to the drive Dad was standing in the front of the garden, throwing the ball for our dog. I quickly went into the house and threw my things in the living room and slowly approached Dad as he was retrieving the ball. I swallowed deeply and then asked the golden question: "Well? How did it go?" Dad stared off into the distance. It was the same lingering stare he made out the window back when we discovered Mum's cancer was terminal. About 5 seconds passed, they were some of the longest, most agonising seconds of my life. He then turned towards me and said bluntly. "I'm going to die."

A small grin then broke out of the corner of his mouth and he hurled the ball and placed his hands on his hips whilst looking up at the sky. "Just like every other fucker on this planet." The doctors had made their decision, the surgery was too high risk. I was of course devastated by the news but this time my outward reaction was different. There was no collapsing to the ground, no weeping and sobbing like there was with Mum. I was 18 now not 14. I just bowed my head solemnly "Oh…" I mumbled. The two of us stood in abject silence for a while before I walked back into the house. I guess a bit like Dad, I had seen so much of death in and around my family that I didn't fear it anymore. When horrific news was brought before me I just became slightly startled at first, then numb to it.

The atmosphere around the house was odd after that. Dad was surprisingly jovial. I guess there's nothing really left to be sad about when the fear of death is removed from you and so he carried on around the house as best as he could. All of us were able to function relatively well in our day to day lives. I threw myself into my studies. My A-Levels were tough but they provided the best form of distraction and my sisters kept things cheery along with Carly who was a constant source of merriment and laughter. One day Dad went into the hospital for a check-up and came out with a confused look on his face.

I probed him as to what could be vexing him so much. He knows he's on limited time, so what's the cause of such bewilderment? "I've just had a word with the doctor there… someone's offered to step up and carry out the procedure." We were all dumbfounded. "I thought it was too risky?" I said quizzically. "Aye, it is. But this man's willing to take the chance." Plans were put in place, and the day rolled around for Dad's big operation. My sisters and I gathered in his room to wish him off and we all gave him a hug. It's only the second time I remember ever giving Dad a hug as an adult. He headed up to Belfast and for the third time in our lives we were all suspended in that horrible vacuum of pondering, not knowing and fearing the worst.

When Anne came in to tell us that the operation was a success we were all mightily relieved. Eventually we were allowed to see him and when we visited him he was lying propped up on the bed all stitched up. He looked dreadful but still alive, still fighting. He could barely talk, and his voice was very strained so we didn't stay too long. When we walked out into the corridor Anne just shook her head. "The man's fucking immortal!" To say this in most terms would be dubbed as an exaggeration, but for my Dad it was closer to an actuality, more so than any other human I have encountered or heard of. To an extent his life reminded me of that of an ancient warrior like Achilles or Theseus.

In the famous myths, their lives too were fraught with peril but just when it looks like the gig's up, one of the Gods who favours them diverts a spear away from their head or provides a hint or guide to aid them on their travels. Given the shit my Dad went through he definitely wasn't favoured by any Gods but the analogy I feel holds a certain weight. Dad told me that although he was in a great deal of pain, he felt liberated after the procedure. He said a crystallising moment for him was when he was facing the patient in the bed opposite and the man had an electronic device that one pushed up against their larynx to speak. He obviously had underwent an operation similar to Dad's. He pushed the device to his neck and groaned out. "It's good…to be alive… today." He then pointed out the window towards the sun that was streaming in and Dad said he felt at peace.

He could not recall to me the name of the doctor who performed the surgery. All he could remember was that with his appearance and accent, he looked to be of Indian descent. I wish I could meet that man and thank him. His courage to stand up and take the burden when no others would is a testimony to all those who are willing to take the reins in a dire situation, and go above and beyond their duty for the good of those in need.

Chapter 37
Dad's Final Chapter

Following the operation Dad was advised to take things slow, even slower than he had before. His musical endeavours had all but ceased as he simply didn't have the strength or stamina to perform at any sort of event, though he still played every Sunday at the chapel and at the odd funeral here and there. He did teach guitar to locals for a while, free of charge. There's a local man named Johnny who I have heard play a number of times in and around the local pubs in Antrim. He's very talented and played alongside my Dad back when he was younger in the showband competitions such as the Fleadh Cheoil and with the Comhaltas. Dad showed him the ropes when he was just starting out, when he was in his early 20's. Throughout the years Dad become known as the go to 'music man' within the parish. He became good friends with another Charlie- Charlie Brogan who was and in fact still is the main co-ordinator of local parish events whether that involves the chapel, GAA or community gatherings and guest speaker nights in the parish hall within Dunloy.

Due to his experience, a few mums were eager for him to give their daughters a chance to showcase their musical talents. They liked the idea of them performing along someone who carried significant weight in the musical set-up within Dunloy, and his knowledge of how to get the best out of young players and singers, no matter what their ability or level of confidence which is why he was getting called up to try out all manners of young fiddle players, guitarists, tin-whistle players and vocalists. The funny thing is, and he would have told you this himself. He had absolutely no qualifications that would have rendered him suitable to teach at any level.

I mentioned earlier in the book that he was familiar with chords and their lettering, but that he never learnt from sheet music in his life. Everything was done by ear which caused him in his later years to became quite disillusioned with how clinical and rigid performers had become. It all had to be carried out according to the way the 'experts' had prescribed it. Everything was to be done to the note and their was no room for any sort of artistic expression or alternate interpretation. Dad told me because of this uncompromising mindset that he flipped in choir practice one evening.

They were trying to learn a hymn, but the singers were struggling to be heard and some were singing in pitches much higher than the rest of them, plus the instruments were clashing and it was just becoming a cacophony of sounds clashing which was anything but the harmonious tone they were trying to exude for a holy mass. Dad made a suggestion. "Right folks, for the ending of the second verse. I say we bring the chord down from a C to a D and we just keep an easy to follow low bass rhythm." Everyone looked at their hymn sheets.

Damien then spoke up. "But, Charlie on here it says that we're to maintain a C chord until the opening verse following the chorus." "I know that" Dad replied. "But we're losing all of our rhythm playing this way and the instrument players are clashing too much with the singers. So I say we change it." The choir began to look around amongst themselves, like a herd of confused sheep that had just been hustled into a pen. Veronica raised her hand. "But, Charlie. It says on the sheet…" "Forget the BLOODY SHEET!" Dad blurted out. They were all taken aback. I've said time and again that Dad was born with a temper but this I think was the first time some of the choir members had seen him explode with rage. He also never liked the idea of music being graded or assessed by judges. "Judges!" He scoffed one day. "I'm playing here nigh on 50 years and when I go to them Fleadh contests I'm being critiqued by some speccy wee twerp who wouldn't know good music if it bit him on the arse."

One day he was finishing up after playing in Sunday mass and a woman came up to him with a load of papers in her hand. She introduced herself as the mother of a young local girl, and was interested in having him listen to his daughter and maybe perform alongside him. She elaborately presented one of the pieces of paper, which turned out to be a certificate. "This is her Grade 8 singing qualification." She then pulled out another. "This is the award she received for coming second with her school in a local districts contest. She also got an A in her GCSE music and…" Dad just graciously started waving his hand. "You don't need to worry about all that, love. If she can sing, she can sing. Tell her to call around next Friday at 7."

For him talent couldn't be chalked down to letters or grades scribbled on a page. He told me that sometimes he thinks singers get carried away by both the grades their teachers give them, and their parents who push them too hard. One day he was in his room with a young girl and her mother, practicing. She was trying to learn an emotional ballad for a wedding and was straining her throat to try and hit a note that was very technical and difficult to strike cleanly. They played through the song a number of times but she continued to sound off-key. Dad said to the young girl. "How about we just take it down a notch cause the note at the end there's a hard one to hit. I say it's safer if you just project at a lower tone." "But she can hit that note!" Her mother snapped. "I've seen her do it numerous times before." It was funny witnessing my Dad interact with people who were more 'educated' than him. He just didn't have time with the frivolities and nonsense that came with breaking everything down into a structure and planning through each point methodically. He just didn't have time for it.

During my Yr 13 parents' evening me and Dad sat down with all my A-Level subject teachers and each one talked about the percentages of each module, the significance of hitting key grading points and saying things like "Tommy's covering the basis of A01, A02 and A04 well, but he needs to remember to include A03 which is contextual information and application to the critical theme of the question." The whole time my Dad just sat back like a college professor listening to a student's thesis, nodding along and going. "Mm-hm. Oh, aye. Yep. Aye, those are important ones Tommy. You've got to be hitting them." When we left the assembly hall I asked him. "Did you understand a single word that came out of their mouths?" Dad shook his head. "Not one fucking notion did I have about what they're on about."

Another great thing about Dad coming through as much as he did is that he got to see his eldest daughter getting married. He wasn't in the best shape but was fit enough to make the trip over to Manchester for Claire's big day. He brought old faithful with him and when we arrived at our digs for the night it wasn't long before he had her whipped out and was strumming along heartily and belting out a few classics whilst Claire and a few of her friends that had gathered were whooping and cheering along.

There's a clip I uploaded onto Facebook as part of my commemoration post for Dad just after he had passed, and it's him sitting on the sofa of the apartment singing 'Knocking on Heaven's Door.' Which was suitably poignant because he spent the majority of our lives, both when we were kids and as adults, knocking on that very door, and he wasn't too be around for too long after that. Despite his considerably weakened condition. He still carried out all of the duties that father of the bride is expected to with fervour and cheer. His wedding speech went down a treat and he was back out in the outside lounge of the hotel with his guitar swung over his shoulder playing away to the adoring crowd. One of Claire's friends who I had never met before came up to me and just went. "Your Dad's a legend."

The years 2019-2021 were among the most bleak for me in living memory because of COVID. The mental strain of being cooped up like we were being sheltered from an air raid was suffocating and both me and my Dad hated it. I remember 2020 was the year I was doing my Masters and it had a crushing impact on my mental health having to complete such an intensive course via Zoom and me and my Dad, as much as we loved one another, were beginning to become irritable and snarky towards one another. It was a difficult time for everyone. Dad was understandably losing more and more of his mobility.

Most of his ventures involved simply sauntering out of his room for a couple of hours and maybe nipping to the bookies if he felt he was strong enough to do it. Then he gradually became more and more ill. He was missing meals and he had the sunken furrowed brow and pale complexion of someone who was slowly ebbing away. It was eventually decided amongst us that he needed to go into hospital. My sister Aine drove him into Causeway and I tagged along in the passenger seat. When we arrived he got out of the car and we each gave him a short hug. He barely had the strength in his legs to carry himself to the hospital entrance. I never knew that when he walked through those doors that he wouldn't be walking back out again. It would be the last time I saw him alive.

As Dad was being treated we continued our mundane routines under the shroud of COVID's vice until one day I began to feel drowsy and my temperature spiked. I took the test and it turned out I had COVID, which meant no leaving the house and living more or less in my room in toxic isolation. About a week or so had passed and we were getting daily updates that Dad was starting to deteriorate. The crushing blow was landed when Claire came to me as I was propped up on the sofa and told me. "He's stopped eating." Which is basically a code word for: his time's almost up. Of course the worst thing about this whole torture, was that I couldn't even see him as he was starting to fade. I was out of bounds to the world. Claire came to me one afternoon, she was staying in the country for a while whilst we tried to sort things out in regards to what had to be put in place for Dad. She informed me that the nurses had told her that Dad was unfortunately on the brink and it was unlikely my COVID would have subsided long enough for me to visit him before he passed.

She asked me if I had a message for him. One last thing I would like to tell him. My eyes began to water and I pondered what I could say that would be suiting. As an English academic I probably could have written a letter about all my memories and how grateful I was for him being around for us as long as he was. I paused for a while as the tears streamed down my face. I began to choke on my words as I strained them out. "Just tell him I love him…and thank you." Claire nodded and said she would pass it on. Part of me was bitter. Bitter towards life. To the fact that I was going to be deprived of my Dad the same way I was with my Mum, without being able to say goodbye properly to their face and receive the closure that I felt would have come from being able to do so.

However, I've learned you can't be angry at fate. Bad things happen and there's nothing you can do about it most of the time and we as humans spend most of our lives just stumbling from one disaster to the next and all we have are our loved ones, and the memories they provide us with that act as fuel to keep us going even after they're gone. Before Claire asked me if I had anything I wanted to say to Dad, it turned out he had one final message for me. It was:

"Tommy's always been good with words. Tell him to use his words."

And's that's just what I did. I used them to tell his story.

THE END

www.ingramcontent.com/pod-product-compliance
Lightning Source LLC
Chambersburg PA
CBHW071207070526
44584CB00019B/2943